FEMINISM AND CHRISTIANITY

Cascade Companions

The Christian theological tradition provides an embarrassment of riches: from Scripture to modern scholarship, we are blessed with a vast and complex theological inheritance. And yet this feast of traditional riches is too frequently inaccessible to the general reader.

The Cascade Companions series addresses the challenge by publishing books that combine academic rigor with broad appeal and readability. They aim to introduce nonspecialist readers to that vital storehouse of authors, documents, themes, histories, arguments, and movements that comprise this heritage with brief yet compelling volumes.

TITLES IN THIS SERIES:

Reading Augustine by Jason Byassee

Conflict, Community, and Honor by John H. Elliott

An Introduction to the Desert Fathers by Jason Byassee

Reading Paul by Michael J. Gorman

Theology and Culture by D. Stephen Long

Creationism and the Conflict over Evolution by Tatha Wiley

Justpeace Ethics by Jarem T. Sawatsky

Reading Bonhoeffer by Geffrey B. Kelly

Theological Interpretation of Scripture by Stephen E. Fowl

FORTHCOMING TITLES:

Christianity and Politics by C. C. Pecknold

iPod, YouTube, Wii Play by D. Brent Laytham

Philippians in Context by Joseph H. Hellerman

Reading Revelation Responsibly by Michael J. Gorman

Feminism and
CHRISTIANITY

Questions and Answers in the Third Wave

CARYN D. RISWOLD

 CASCADE *Books* • Eugene, Oregon

FEMINISM AND CHRISTIANY
Questions and Answers in the Third Wave

Cascade Companions

Cascade Books
A Division of Wipf and Stock Publishers
199 W. 8th Ave., Suite 3
Eugene, OR 97401

www.wipfandstock.com

ISBN 13: 978-1-55635-837-1

Cataloging-in-Publication data:

Riswold, Caryn D.

   Feminism and Christianity : questions and answers in the third wave /
Caryn D. Riswold.

   ISBN 13: 978-1-55635-837-1

   viii + 136 p. ; 20 cm. Includes bibliographical references.

   1. Feminist theology. 2. Feminism—Religious aspects—Christianity.
3. Women and religion. 4. Women in Christianity. I. Title. II. Series.

BT83.55 R579 2009

Manufactured in the U.S.A.

Contents

Acknowledgments

This book was born out of a conversation I had with K. C. Hanson at Cascade Books, who described to me the recently launched Cascade Companions series—short, accessible books designed to introduce a wider reading audience to topics and texts in the study of religion. That discussion, combined with an impending sabbatical from teaching at Illinois College (IC) led me to conceive of a basic text revisiting some fundamental questions between feminism and Christianity in this generation. I am grateful both to K. C. for asking the question, and to Illinois College for granting the sabbatical that led to the completion of this book.

My daily interactions with undergraduate students over the past nine years have pushed me to try making complicated and often controversial topics both interesting and understandable. I regularly encounter wonderful students who are hesitant to be critical of their Christianity, and great young people who are not convinced that feminism has any relevance in their lives. When we spend a semester or two together, I am humbled to be part of their discovery of the joys and burdens of thinking about their faith and comprehending the very real need for feminism in our world today.

The voices and faces of my IC students have been very much with me as I wrote this book.

In addition, I have had fruitful and productive conversations with several of my colleagues at Illinois College about this book: Kelly Dagan, Lisa Udel, and Robert Kunath read early drafts and provided detailed constructive feedback and reactions, while Steve Gardner and Karen Dean were part of lively conversations about the project. Reverend Rebecca Gordon shared her wisdom and her life with me from the very inception of the project, as she has for over a decade now. A marvelous group of women—Lisa Udel, Beth Capo, Jenny Brown, Rev. Kara Baylor, and Rev. Rebecca Gordon—gave me the earliest suggestions for questions and topics to cover. Many other experiences with colleagues and friends have put me right in the middle of the relationship between feminism and Christianity for years. I am honored to learn with all these people.

My first reader and generous companion throughout life is Mark Schelske, and his wit and commitment to the writing life sustain me every moment. I am finally interested in acknowledging two toddler feminists, Emma and Amelia, who came into my friends' families while I was generating this project. Thinking about their lives and seeing their faces propels me to work making the world more just and joyful every day.

Introduction

Personal Introduction

I travel through the rural Midwest proudly wearing a black T-shirt proclaiming in hot-pink letters: This is What a Feminist Looks Like. The manager of the Cracker Barrel in Missouri said to my husband: "She doesn't look any different than my wife."

My family heritage is intimately tied up with Lutheran congregations in South Dakota, and I was in the first generation of our family who earned a college degree. When I was about to head across the country to graduate school, the pastor of my home church remarked about my interest in feminist theology: "But you're not one of those feminazis, right?"

During a much more recent summer, a friend of mine introduced me as a feminist theologian to her father-in-law, a pastor in a mainline Protestant denomination for the past forty years, and he later asked her, "So, what *are* the basic tenets of feminist theology?"

In the same weekend, I attended and presented a paper at the National Women's Studies Association, where I found, other than in my own sparsely attended session, virtually no papers on Christianity or any other specific religion, with only various relatively vague discussions about some amorphous spirituality.

Later that summer, I was a speaker at a national gathering of theologians in a mainline Protestant denomination. During the question-and-answer session, I found myself reminding the audience that the problem leading to women's oppression around the globe is still patriarchy.

Some theologians, and perhaps some denominations, reflect a comment made by Catherine Keller in a recent article: that feminism "may have become overfamiliar before it ever got familiar."[1] Because of the advances women have made in society and even in some churches in recent generations, the work of feminism is sometimes seen as over and done: mission accomplished.

This array of episodes suggested to me that a lot of serious Christians and serious feminists do not actually know much about each other in the twenty-first century. Maybe they don't care about each other. Maybe they think they don't need to pay attention to each other any more. They clearly are not really talking or listening to each other. The rich and varied field of feminist theology that has emerged in the past forty years has demonstrated that they are compatible: Rosemary Radford Ruether, Delores S. Williams, Elisabeth Schüssler Fiorenza, Ada María Isasi-Díaz, Phyllis Trible, Jacquelyn Grant, and Elizabeth Johnson among many others show how women working from a decidedly feminist perspective engage deeply with the resources of the Christian tradition to both deconstruct and reconstruct its theology. Mary Daly, Carol Christ, and others show how feminist critique of the Christian tradition often leads women away from it.

1. Keller, "The Apophasis of Gender," 906.

At the same time, many Protestant denominations have faithfully responded to feminism and the women's movement by changing their practices of ordination and appointment to the ministry to include women, by using inclusive language for God throughout the life of the church, by expanding liturgical resources to be more inclusive in prayer and hymnody, by opening worship and congregational leadership to lay women and men, and by issuing social statements on topics like abortion, contraception, and sexuality that allow women and families to exercise their own moral discernment. Feminism and Christianity can learn and have learned a lot from and with each other.

This book asks and answers some fundamental questions that Christians and feminists have about each other in a new century and a new generation. The questions reflect suspicions encountered in a meeting of the two, and the answers reflect the twenty-first-century realities that now inform both. It is time for a renewed conversation between feminism and Christianity if anyone inside or outside the two groups thinks that either is no longer relevant. Feminism has transformed the lives of women and men irrevocably, and Christianity remains a powerful and ever-changing tradition with enormous influence around the world. Before explaining these things more closely by getting to the questions and answers, some history and basic terminology needs to be explained.

TERMINOLOGY AND HISTORY

A problem with this conversation is that both feminism and Christianity are not monolithic entities. Both have been "essentialized" in the sense that many assume that *Christian* means only one essential thing, and that *feminist* means only one essential thing. Many think that all feminists are alike, and that all Christians are alike. Neither has ever been true. Feminism and its goals have been defined differently by different individuals and groups at different points throughout history, and different types of feminism continue to exist. Christianity has been a diverse and complicated religious and social entity from its earliest community of believers, and different types of Christianity still flourish in the twenty-first century. Both feminism and Christianity are traditions in the original sense of the Latin root word, *trado*, literally a "handing over" of something. Traditions grow and shift and change as they are handed over throughout time and across generations while retaining insight from the past. Both feminism and Christianity are traditions that continue to change, making this renewed conversation necessary and possible.

Feminism

Feminism criticizes sexism and patriarchy, and advocates for the equal humanity of women. This basic definition is assumed throughout this book. Feminism entails both a critical and a constructive component: patriarchy is criticized, and women's equal humanity is constructed. Core beliefs of feminism include the idea of human equality, alongside an activist impulse to do something to establish social and political justice for women where it has not fully existed. Students of history generally discuss feminism using the metaphor of waves: first-wave, second-wave, and third-wave feminism are largely generational movements distinguished on the basis of historical situation, goals, and strategies, among other things. A brief review of this history reveals how feminism has shifted over time and leads to a discussion of the different types of feminism that exist today.

History of Feminism

The first wave of feminism encompasses the work of women and men in the nineteenth century to gain for women the right to vote. It dovetailed with abolitionism since many of the early suffragists were also working to end slavery in the United States. The nineteenth century produced women like Sarah Grimke, Elizabeth Cady Stanton, and Matilda Joslyn Gage, who advocated for women's rights at home and in their government, who spoke out against the institution of slavery, who criticized the Christian church, and who produced classic texts such as *Letters on the Equality of the Sexes* (1838) and *The Woman's Bible* (1898).

The first wave of feminism was led almost entirely by white, upper-class women. The 2004 movie *Iron-Jawed Angels* tells the story of some of these women and includes two dramatized moments that reveal historical truths about race and class. In one scene, Ida B. Wells-Barnett, an African American woman activist who worked to end lynching around the U.S., demands that the black women march with the white women in their demonstration for the vote on Woodrow Wilson's inauguration day, not in a separate section. In another scene, Alice Paul, founder of the National Woman's Party and author of the original Equal Rights Amendment, attempts to recruit women factory workers for the cause of suffrage. Labor activist Ruza Wenclawska directly challenges Paul about the relevance of the vote for the lives of women working seven days a week under excruciating conditions in the factory.

Moments like this reveal some of the criticism of first-wave feminism that has since emerged: In their focus on the vote, these early feminist activists were nearly blind to the realities of life for women of color and working-class women. This women's movement was populated by women who were racially segregated and socially privileged. Their focus was narrowly on achieving the right to vote, which they believed would improve life for all women equally. The first wave of feminism culminated in the ultimate ratification of the Nineteenth Amendment, guaranteeing women the right to vote in 1920.

The second wave of feminism surfaced beginning in the middle of the twentieth century. With the Food and Drug Administration approval of oral contraception in 1960 and the proliferation of social and civil rights movements throughout the 1960s, feminism emerged in this generation focused on issues like women's reproductive health, an equal-rights amendment to the Constitution, access to educational resources (secured with Title IX in 1972), and social problems like sexual harassment and workplace discrimination. The 1970s produced women theologians such as Mary Daly and Rosemary Radford Ruether, who advocated for women's rights, spoke out against the Vietnam War, and produced theological texts like *Beyond God the Father* (1973) and *Sexism and God-Talk* (1983).

Like the first wave of feminism, the second wave too was dominated by white women, and by educated upper- and middle-class women. This did not go unnoticed and did not last unchallenged for long. Writer and activist Audre Lorde was among the first to publically call white feminists to task for their continued erasure of poor women and women of color from the women's movement. In 1981 at a national women's studies conference, she pointed out that "white women ignore their built-in privilege of whiteness and define woman in terms of their own experience alone."[2] She also challenged feminists directly saying, "it is a particular academic arrogance to assume any discussion of feminist theory without examining our many differences, and without a significant input from poor women, Black and Third World women, and lesbians."[3] Lorde thus opened the way for real criticism of feminism and its attempts to speak of "women's experience" without attending to the many differences of experience that women have on the basis of race, class, sexuality, age, ability, and other factors.

What many now call the third wave of feminism is generally populated by those of us who learned about feminism with the critiques of Audre Lorde and were raised on the benefits of first- and second-wave feminist activism. For me, there have always been girls' sports and boys' sports in school. Women and men my age were raised with *Free to Be You and Me*, with racial integration on *Sesame Street*, with legal and safe birth control, with basic access to the higher-education institutions of our choosing, and with the presence of women pastors and priests throughout much of the Christian tradition. Third-wave feminists focus on a myriad of social problems like safeguarding marriage equality, ending race- and gender-based violence, ameliorating the effects of global capitalism on the poorest of poor women, and ensuring that the gains made for women's equality in previous generations are not lost in shifting political and ideological

2. Lorde, "Age, Race, Class, and Sex," 117.
3. Lorde, "The Master's Tools," 110.

winds. Third-wave feminists also continue to advocate for benefits that still elude women (such as equal pay for equal work), and work to uncover sexist ideologies that are often more subversive than ever before.

Jennifer Baumgardner and Amy Richards in their 2000 book *Manifesta* point out that feminists in the third wave have inherited a "core belief in the legal, political, and social equality" from the first wave, along with "strategies to fight sexual harassment, domestic abuse, the wage gap" and other issues from the second wave. Beyond that, modern problems have been added to the mix: "equal access to the Internet and technology, HIV/AIDS awareness, child sexual abuse, self-mutilation, globalization, eating disorders, body image, sexual health, and access to adoption and legal marriage.[4] One arena in which third-wave feminism has not had a sustained focus is religion, though some voices are beginning to emerge. Joy Ann McDougall discusses "Feminist Theology for a New Generation" in her 2005 article in *The Christian Century*, and describes the features of a new feminist theology. It includes the "mainstreaming of feminist discourse" to address broader social issues like globalization, work and family patterns, as well as the central doctrines of the Christian church.[5] Third-wave feminist theology is still taking shape today.

Types of Feminism

In addition to this ebb and flow of issues throughout the generations, various types of feminism have emerged with different theoretical frameworks and different terms to focus their

4. Baumgardner and Richards, *Manifesta*, 21.
5. McDougall, "Feminist Theology for a New Generation," 20-25.

analyses of sex and gender. Feminist theories that emerged most strongly during the second wave locate the explanation for sexism and its solution in different places. *Marxist feminists* adopt the theories of production and critiques of capitalism, that Karl Marx developed in the nineteenth century, to understand the source of women's oppression by locating it within a system of economic and class stratification. *Socialist feminists* attempt to merge this class analysis with a more focused gender analysis to explain sexism.

Liberal feminists argue primarily that since a major source of women's oppression is unequal treatment under the law, changing the law and transforming the current social system is the most effective way to eradicate women's oppression. *Radical feminists* see gender oppression as the initial and fundamental form of oppression. *Cultural feminists* examine the differences between men and women and revalidate that which patriarchy has devalued: all things associated with the female and the feminine. *Gynocentric feminists* argue that the differences between men and women are so significant that women's separatism is the most desired outcome. A less radical form of this is *difference feminism*, which is more neutral about the need to separate men and women and seeks to provide explanations and context for understanding the differences that do exist.

Throughout this book I am articulating what could be called a third-wave liberal feminist view of the relationship between feminism and Christianity. This means that I have come to feminism within the second wave, benefitting and learning from it while turning my attention to the complex issues of the twenty-first century that demand our simultaneous engagement with race and gender and class and sexuality and many other factors. It also means that I am generally committed to working within existing systems and institutions in order to make them better for women and men. These include politics, education, and religion.

At the same time, I take seriously much of the radical-feminist critique which would advocate abandoning patriarchal religion altogether. I am informed by the Marxist-feminist critique that social class is a fundamental source of oppression, and I see that the cultural-feminist move to prize women's humanity as unique and distinct from men's humanity has been a source for women's empowerment in various communities throughout history. My choice to articulate a feminism of one sort does not diminish the insight and power of feminisms of other sorts.

Christianity

Christianity is a religion whose adherents believe that God is uniquely revealed in the person of Jesus, who is the Christ, the Messiah and Savior for the world. Core beliefs of Christianity, in addition to the belief about Jesus as the Christ, include the belief that human beings are uniquely created in the image of God; that they are redeemed in a sinful and fallen world by a loving and compassionate God who wants abundant and peaceable life for all; and that they are sustained by the Spirit of the God, who relates to them throughout their lives. Christians believe that this triune God's grace is unearned, and that their faith is most active in love. Christianity has always been a diverse religion—from the early divisions between Pauline Christians and gnostic Christians through the Great Schism and the Reformation to the modern proliferation of

Protestant denominations, new Christian movements, and independent megachurches.

The history of the religion, as well as its current variations, shows how despite the fact of core beliefs, many different Christianities exist today.

History of Christianity

Following the life and death of Jesus, whose followers proclaimed him to be the resurrected Christ, the earliest Christian communities in the first century were divided about many issues. Some of these issues included the relationship of Christianity to Judaism, from which it emerged; and how one was to gain knowledge of the God proclaimed by Jesus and his followers. Jewish Christians believed that the Jesus movement was fundamentally about reform within their long-standing tradition, while Pauline Christians believed that justification was a product of God's grace, available to all who had faith and not just to Jews. Other movements like gnostic Christianity understood the teachings of Jesus in conjunction with other philosophical ideas like *gnosis*, or special knowledge. Pauline Christianity won the struggle to define Christianity in these early generations, appealing as it did to a broad range of people: Jews and Gentiles alike, along with women, the poor and the marginalized. The early phase of Christianity as a fledgling movement came to an end with the Edict of Milan, issued by Constantine in 313. The Edict ended persecution of Christians and made a way for the eventual elevation of the movement to the preferred and official religion of the Roman Empire.

From the fourth century through the fifteenth century, Christianity became a powerful world religion with fully articulated creeds, doctrines, and dogmas to which adherents were required to express allegiance. An institution that centralized church authority—the papacy—was established, and an early conflict ended in the Great Schism of 1054 when the Eastern churches and Western churches split over issues of leadership (the pope in Rome or the patriarch in Constantinople?), language (Latin or Greek?), and the biblical canon (which books are in, and which books are out). The mutual excommunication of the leaders in the Eastern Orthodox and Western Catholic churches revealed that Christianity had become a religion with growing complications.

By the time the fifteenth century arrived, Roman Christianity had come to dominate western Europe, and criticisms of its central institutions and practices were emerging on a number of fronts. John Wycliffe and others had initiated movements to translate the Bible into local languages, rather than to maintain only the scholars' and priests' Latin; and the church's increasing reliance on indulgences as a matter of promise to the faithful and a financial resource for the institution began to draw criticism. It was against a shifting social and political landscape that Martin Luther emerged in Germany. He was an Augustinian monk deeply concerned about the state of his own soul as well as the soul of the church. When he posted his Ninety-five Theses at Wittenberg in 1517, he was well on his way to recovering the biblical themes from Paul's letters to the Romans and the Galatians—that everyone is justified by grace through faith in Christ. The impact of this reclaimed biblical theme was a sweeping Reformation. This Reformation altered how people experienced worship, how they understood the grace of God, and how they read their Bibles. The Catholic Counter-Reformation rejected the Protestant movement fully at the Council of Trent in 1545, reaffirming the Latin Vulgate as official church Scripture, rearticulating a theology of seven sacraments after as many as five had been irrevocably stripped of that status by the Reformers, and closing the door on other Protestant criticisms of the institution and its practices.

As Christianity took shape after the Reformation, denominations began to proliferate when there were disagreements about issues like infant baptism, the permissibility of war, and the proper relationship between church and state. Through the Enlightenment and into the modern era, philosophers and sociologists both welcomed and dismissed the globally dominant Christianity. Such Christianity on one hand resisted and on the other hand responded to new developments in science and the study of history—developments that fundamentally challenged basic tenets of Christian belief such as who wrote the Bible, and when and how the world came into existence.

Two final distinguishing events have brought Christianity into the form it is largely in today. The establishment of the World Council of Churches in 1948 represented an intentional move toward a global Christian community in the wake of World War II and the Holocaust. This organization continues to engage its member Christian churches in the global community, a task that becomes even more pressing over time. The Second Vatican Council represented a similar move to bring the Roman Catholic Church into conversation with issues of the twentieth century. Called by Pope John XXIII in 1962, the series of council meetings over three years discussed issues raised by the modern world: what it meant to be human in the twentieth century, what it meant to be church in a world that could no longer function as if

Christianity were the only truth, how to assess the church's culpability after two world wars and the Holocaust, and what would happen with the growing collapse of colonialism in lands where the church had evangelized. Vatican II produced a number of groundbreaking documents and statements that articulated the place of the Church in this world, that shaped worship life for a new generation of Catholics, and that left a number of questions (such as the possible place of women in Church leadership) answered in a way that was unsatisfying for legions of the faithful.

Types of Christianity

With this history, Christianity remains today a complicated religion with many different expressions, some of which dispute the legitimacy of others. Several ways of categorizing types of Christianity exist and have varying levels of specificity. The broadest and most basic typology that emerges from the brief history sketched above names Catholic, Orthodox, and Protestant as the major forms of Christianity today.

The Roman Catholic Church is the organization that claims that its leader, the pope, is the apostolic successor of St. Peter, appointed by Jesus to be the head of his church on earth. The Orthodox traditions are those that originated largely from the East-West split and the Great Schism of the eleventh century. Many subgroups fall under the category of Orthodox today—from Russian Orthodox to Assyrian Orthodox to Greek Orthodox. Protestant traditions are perhaps the most numerous, originating with the sixteenth-century Reformation and leading to hundreds or even thousands of denominations today.

What the Catholic-Orthodox-Protestant taxonomy does not completely account for in present-day Christianity is the emergence of groups like restorationist churches and independent Bible churches, many of which claim to be returning to the foundations of the religion or restoring a lost history of Christianity altogether. In fact, the Great Awakening of the eighteenth century in the United States laid the groundwork for communities like Joseph Smith's Latter-day Saints and Mary Baker Eddy's Christian Scientists to undercut existing religious institutions and traditions with renewed spiritual fervor and with followers who adhere to these teachings still. Throughout the twentieth century, evangelicalism in America began to reshape not only the religious but also the political landscape in ways that continue to affect culture and law in the twenty-first century.

Throughout this book, I speak from the position of one reared and educated in a mainline Protestant denomination in the United States: the Evangelical Lutheran Church in America. This affects my understanding of what it means to be Christian, and what Christianity looks like. My advanced degrees are from Protestant schools, both Lutheran and Methodist, and my nine years of teaching have been at a university and a college related to Protestant denominations: Lutheran, Presbyterian, and United Church of Christ. Therefore this book reflects the view of a scholar and person shaped by a certain intellectual and family traditions. At the same time, my views are informed by the rigorous scholarship of Catholic women and men, challenged by conservative evangelical Christian students, and accountable to the questions of those agnostic and atheist friends whom religious communities ignore or dismiss too easily.

FEMINISM AND CHRISTIANITY

All this makes the notion of a book about basic questions between *feminism* and *Christianity* essentially complicated. If neither word means just one thing, then how can a dialogue between the two spheres be focused enough to have any meaning?

By embracing the diversity that is feminism and the variations that are Christianity, this book originates from my own feminist and Christian location and reaches in a number of directions to bring many people into a renewed conversation for the twenty-first century. For Christians who think that the goals of feminism have been achieved and that feminists should stop complaining, this book will serve as a reality check about the situation for women today and as a push to think more deeply about the inequality and injustices very real in churches and communities around the world. For feminists who think that Christianity is not worth their attention because it remains an oppressive institution after so many generations of feminist activism, this book will serve as a reality check about the need for continued criticism as well as about the liberating and life-giving dimensions of a religion that has sustained women and their survival across time and cultures.

Feminism and Christianity both exist as powerful cultural and political forces in the twenty-first century. A deeper understanding of each in relation to the other suggests that there are ongoing conflicts as well as unexplored areas of common interest and cause. For some, this is an old and obvious point. To them, I ask why suspicions remain and why the work of creating a just society and more equitable church eludes us. For others, this is a problematic claim—that the two could work together. To them, I encourage further reading and reflection as to whether their conclusion is based in reality or in stereotype.

A Readers' Guide

The questions and answers that follow attempt to cover a range of topics fundamental to a discussion between feminism and Christianity. By no means do these exhaust all the questions and answers that exist between the two. In fact, I encourage readers to come up with additional questions for their own consideration and conversation. I attempt to be comprehensive while clearly not exhausting the details on any one point. To this end, because the essays in this book are relatively concise, I have provided a short list of suggested readings associated with each topic at the end of each essay. These are texts and authors that inform my claims as well as provide much additional material for discussion. I encourage anyone or any group reading this book to pursue topics of special interest to them by seeking out more authors and texts, starting with the ones I mention. In addition, I have provided a glossary of key terms and concepts at the end of the book, which I encourage all readers to consult. With the glossary I have included a summary list of the questions and answers for easy reference.

The book is structured so that an individual, group, or class could dip in and out of it as interest and time permit. The first half of the book looks at feminist questions to Christianity. It is written to address the questions from feminists suspicious of Christianity. It could be of special interest to feminist activists and women's studies students.

The second half of the book looks at Christian questions to feminism and is written to address questions from Christians suspicious of feminism. It could be of special interest to individual Christians and their congregational reading and study groups. In both cases, the questions will hopefully provoke more questions and further discussion in response to the answers I have composed. However readers approach this book, I beg each one to keep reading and to keep talking to those of whom they are suspicious or with whom they are unfamiliar. I am a teacher by vocation and intend this book to be provocative as well as educational.

SUGGESTED READING

Sally Bruyneel and Alan G. Padgett. *Introducing Christianity.* 2003.

Estelle Freedman, *No Turning Back: The History of Feminism and the Future of Women.* 2003.

ONE

Feminist Questions of Christianity

Feminists are often suspicious of Christianity and have a lot of questions about a religion led by men that worships a male God. In what way can this religion be good for women and men who are interested in an equal humanity? History provides many examples of the ways that Christianity has served to support and justify patriarchal ideas like wifely submission and women's second-class status. With the weight of this evidence, feminists wonder why they should continue to care about Christianity. Perhaps it is only another patriarchal institution that needs to be dismantled.

The questions in this section capture this critical attitude toward Christianity, and the answers provide some information about the religion in a way that takes the questions seriously, often recognizing where the suspicions are well grounded. Some of the influence that feminism has already had on Christianity is discussed, and attention is paid to the real ways that Christianity has been good for many women. In addition, the questions and answers in this section account for the fact that a global Christianity exists today in a deeply connected, multifaith world.

The answers in this section do not presume to defend Christianity at every point, but they do presume that Christianity is something worth paying attention to, and worth challenging and reforming. Feminists have rarely backed down from a challenge, and engaging with Christianity is one of them that the third wave is ready to face.

1.1 WHY SHOULD FEMINISTS CARE ABOUT CHRISTIANITY?

Feminists should care about Christianity because it is simultaneously a religion with an egalitarian vision that has been and should continue to be liberating for women, and because it has been a major institution of patriarchy that remains a pervasive cultural force needing criticism. The first two waves of feminism demonstrated how various institutions of patriarchy promoted injustice and inequality especially for women, and they helped bring about positive change in many of them. The work of criticizing the negative elements of Christianity while uncovering its positive legacy must continue today with third-wave feminist insights and strategies.

One reason that feminists should care about Christianity is that it impacts women's lives in a significant way. It was during the second wave of feminism that activists and scholars began turning their attention to religion in a more sustained and sophisticated way than the suffragists had in the previous century. In the United States, this meant paying particular attention to Christianity. Early feminist theological works challenging the church as well as its ideas were written by Valerie Saiving and Mary Daly. Saiving offered the first critique of basic Christian ideas about sin, while Daly mounted a serious case against the Catholic Church for its treatment of women throughout history. They saw that like government, education, and the professional world, religion was a power-ful tool of patriarchy that needed challenge and reform.

Because Christianity is a religion that helps perpetuate patriarchy, whether or not a woman participates in a religious community, whether or not she is religious at all, religion affects her life because it shapes society. In any society, the dominance of one religion necessarily affects the culture and the laws that impact everyone. Despite the legal separation of church and state that defines religious freedom in the United States, Christianity is a dominant cultural force: every president to date has been a Christian; the vast majority of Supreme Court justices to date have been Christian; about 77 percent of the American public calls itself Christian.[1] This is one reason why, whether religious or not, feminists need to engage in the critical examination necessary to understand Christianity.

Effects of this cultural dominance of Christianity are seen in several events from recent years: Controversy erupted in several states when pharmacists refused to fill prescrip-tions for emergency contraception, written by medical doctors, on the claim that it violated their religious beliefs against contraception and/or abortion. Much of the anti-choice and anti-abortion activism in America has its roots in Christian communities; the 2008 election saw the passage of Proposition 8 in California, which revoked the right of gay and lesbian Americans in that state to marry. This resulted in widespread protests and demonstrations targeting Mormons and evangelical Christian churches, groups who publically support outlawing gay marriage and who helped fund the

1. Kosmin, et al., "The American Religious Identification Survey," 10.

Proposition 8 campaign. These examples show what many feminists consider to be the negative, sexist, and homophobic legacy of Christianity. Because it is a patriarchal institution, in practice as well as in its belief, that supports legal and political maneuvers to limits on rights based on gender, it necessarily commands attention from feminists. But that is not the only reason.

Feminists should care about Christianity because it provides life and spiritual sustenance for many women. This has been true from the days that Jesus talked with, healed, and dined with women, and it is still true today. Feminist biblical scholars like Elisabeth Schüssler Fiorenza help Christians more fully understand the relevance of Jesus' own actions with regard to women. She suggests that there were feminist impulses within Judaism that Jesus amplified in his teaching and ministry. Scholars of the Pauline literature show some of the egalitarian impulses of that early Christian community, and how they were sidelined as the church grew and gained power into the fourth century. The inclusion of commendations and greetings for women like Phoebe ("minister of the church"), Prisca ("who work[s] with me in Christ Jesus"), and Junia ("prominent among the apostles") at the conclusion of Paul's letter to the Romans (Romans 16:1, 3, 7), for example, suggests a gender ideology different from what many see in texts from 1 Timothy and Ephesians that restrict women's public and teaching authority. Patriarchy ultimately defined the institution of Christianity due in no small measure to the cultural and philosophical influences of the society in which it emerged and took formal shape. Historians like Karen Torjesen, however, have meticulously shown how traditions such as women priests were in fact part of Christianity from the beginning.

Beyond the early formative years and texts of Christianity, women's voices show how the religion continued to provide a source of life and liberation even as patriarchy took an entrenched hold on it. Medieval women mystics and martyrs give powerful testimony to the way visions of God and Jesus sustained them throughout their lives. Julian of Norwich's intimate descriptions of the Mother Jesus and Catherine of Siena's passionate engagement with the politics of the thirteenth-century church provide models of women who seized their voice because of their religious experiences. Surviving narratives from slaves in the American historical record reveal further how biblical stories like the exodus provided the spark of hope that God was on the side of the enslaved, how Jesus was seen as the one who suffered like they did, and that there was liberation and new life awaiting them.

If there is something good in Christianity, which legions of women and men throughout history and in the world today suggest, then feminist scholars have reason to pay attention to it. If there continues to be something problematic in the religion, which legions of critics and scholars suggest, then feminists have an obligation to engage it critically. This obligation includes bringing the most serious critical feminist tools to bear on Christian beliefs and practices. This can contribute to chipping away the patriarchal mantle and liberating a core message that early on declared that ethnicity, sex, and status do not ultimately determine one's fate: "There is no longer Jew or Greek, there is no longer slave or free, there is no longer male and female; for all of you are one in Christ Jesus" (Galatians 3:28). This fundamental Christian belief is that everyone has access to salvation through grace and faith. The idea that can be embraced by feminism here is the preservation and affirmation of the equal humanity of all people regardless of gender, race, or class.

Christianity in the twenty-first century and feminism in the third wave share a world with increasingly complicated social and spiritual problems. If contemporary feminists are concerned about the many factors that shape women's and men's lives today—like race, class, gender, sexuality, age, ability, and education level—then religion must also be addressed as one of these factors. Third-wave feminists have learned from and widely embraced many social and political strategies of previous generations. The attention that Christianity and its theology received throughout the second wave needs to be revitalized with new insights about the complexities of human life. Feminists in the third wave have a responsibility to rearticulate the criticisms of Christianity for those who have not yet fully understood them, as well as an opportunity to reshape theology for a world confronting new social and political challenges: more than a billion people living in poverty worldwide, a climate changing around us dramatically, a faltering global economy whose failure disproportionately affects the poorest among us, and proliferating international conflicts. Feminism can continue to show how religions like Christianity have been part of the problem and must become part of the solution.

Feminism should reform Christianity to establish and maintain women's equal humanity while confronting the ways that patriarchy continues to maintain male dominance over women.

Suggested Reading

Elizabeth A. Clark and Herbert Richardson, editors. *Women and Religion: The Original Sourcebook of Women in Christian Thought.* 1996.

Mary Daly. *The Church and the Second Sex.* 1968.

Elisabeth Schüssler Fiorenza. *In Memory of Her: A Feminist Theological Reconstruction of Christian Origins.* 1983.

Karen Jo Torjesen. *When Women Were Priests: Women's Leadership in the Early Church and the Scandal of their Subordination in the Rise of Christianity.* 1993.

1.2 How Has Christianity Been a Problem for Women?

Feminist criticism of Christianity looks at its history, its social and political influence, and its theology for the ways that it has harmed women. In fact, as is the case with several social institutions, Christianity has been both the problem and the solution in the lives of many women. By understanding in more detail key aspects of Christianity, feminists can understand the complicated legacy that it presents for women and men today. The sexist and even violent legacy of Christianity must be named, challenged, and changed. This is precisely where feminists are among those most important to reorienting the religion toward justice.

A brief look into the history of Christianity shows how its view of women sits at the root of much social and theological sexism. Tertullian, while instructing women and men on how to dress in the third century, told women that they were the devil's gateway, the means by which evil entered the world.

He articulated the part of traditional Christian anthropology that views women as responsible for sin and evil entering the world because of Eve's actions in the Garden of Eden story of Genesis 3. This idea of some ancient and primordial human decision has had a tremendous influence not only on Christianity's view of women but on dominant Western cultural ideas about women and men.

In addition, ancient misunderstandings of biology were woven into medieval Scholastic texts in a way that continues to misshape our understandings of sex and gender. Saint Thomas Aquinas's theological views of human nature reflected his thirteenth-century understanding of the process of procreation, borrowed from Aristotle: man supplies the form and the ideal representation of human being, and woman is merely the matter and the place where the form grows. To put it more crudely, with ejaculation, the man implants a very tiny person (the homunculus) into the woman who is little more than the warm place for the tiny person to grow. The nineteenth-century discovery of the ovum and subsequent realizations about how procreation actually takes place rendered this understanding of human beings irrelevant. In many ways, however, the assumptions and dualisms about men and women derived from it remain in place. Aristotelian biology and Aquinas's theological adoption of it provided a foundation for claims about male superiority that still exist: Men are superior, women are inferior; men are stronger, women are weaker; men are active and women are passive; men provide, women receive; men create, women participate.

Ideas like these from the intellectual history of Christianity reveal where some of the roots of sexism and misogyny lie. Feminists who have an understanding of this can simultaneously point out the errors insofar as they exist, and they can push the religion and society toward better articulations of what it means to be human. Knowing specifically why Christianity has been a problem for women with these historical notes enables feminists to participate in fixing the problem.

The social and political implications of Christianity also deserve attention insofar as the religion has been oppressive for women both inside and outside the church. In the Western world, Christianity has been the religion of the dominant classes, and as such it has provided ideological basis for many of its oppressive practices. Biblical texts have been used to support the notion that wives must submit to their husbands, and that slaves should obey their masters. Arguments presented in the early twentieth century against women gaining the right to vote in places like Britain and the United States relied heavily on assumptions drawn from Christian ideas about men and women, like those described above. The idea that women were fully dependent on and represented by their husbands under the law stems in part from a reading of Genesis 2, where the woman is made from the rib of the man. The subsequent claim that women are physically inferior to men is also connected to the flawed biology and philosophical presumptions about form and matter from Aristotle and Aquinas. Dualisms borrowed in part from gnostic and Platonic philosophy also influenced the increasingly patriarchal Christianity to value spiritual over physical, free over slave, form over matter, and male over female. Patriarchy still depends on this mode of thinking to maintain the unquestioned dominance of men over women.

Despite some core theological commitments to peace, justice, and compassion, Christianity has also justified violence against women, officially as well as subtly. This is where feminist critique of sexism in Christian theology becomes essential. Official sanction of violence against women occurred with the persecution and subsequent execution of women as witches in the fifteenth and sixteenth centuries. This enterprise was supported by a declaration from Pope Innocent VIII, and led by Heinrich Kramer and Jacob Sprenger, who authored the *Malleus Mallificarum* (the *Hammer against Witches*) in 1486. This text, a manual for finding and dealing with witches, excessively focused on women's sexuality and women's involvement in things mysterious to many men, like miscarriages and stillbirths. It reflected the Christian theological views of women and sex promoted by Tertullian, Augustine, and Aquinas as described above. These Christian thinkers fundamentally believed that women were inferior beings more susceptible to the influence of the devil in part because of the demands of their bodies.

Historians conservatively estimate that sixty thousand people were executed during the medieval witch persecutions, a majority of them women; and some scholars estimate that millions were brought to trial.[2] This massive tragedy was among other things a culmination of generations of misogyny and misunderstanding about women perpetuated in large part by the Christian church.

Such sexism still exists today when well-intentioned pastors and Christian neighbors counsel women to endure mistreatment at their husbands' hands in the spirit of turning the other cheek, or pressure a woman to prematurely forgive her rapist, or persuade a woman not to file charges against an abuser because of how it will affect his life. Darice Jones provides one such personal narrative:

2. Clark and Richardson, "Woman as Witch," 119–43.

> But my greatest lesson about the value of women in the church's eyes was a personal one. One of those pulpit kings took off his crown and robe and stepped down from his dais just long enough to rape me . . . When I confided in my trusted women in the church, they told me my salvation depended on me forgiving him. Years later when I told our pastor, he told me that the preacher had much more to protect and much more to lose if the news became public. He was a man with a family. I was just a girl.[3]

Theological justification for counsel like this comes in part from biblical texts ("wives be subject to your husbands as you are to the Lord," Ephesians 5:22) as well as from sexist religious culture. Carole R. Bohn has called this a "theology of ownership" that has promoted male dominion over all things, again based on a reading of the Genesis texts. In cases of child abuse by priests, a theology of ownership again paves the way for destructive actions. Once experiences like these are revealed and taken seriously, such justifications can be delegitimized. The more that women find the courage and support to tell their stories and hold their religious leaders to account, the fewer women and children there will be who receive such warped counsel. As the movement built on the very criterion of taking women's experience seriously, feminism has a crucial role to play in making such truths known and such actions and theological claims unacceptable within Christianity, holding it accountable to wider cultural parameters and critique.

3. Jones, "Falling Off the Tightrope," 140.

Many Christians, both female and male, who want the justice orientation of the religion reclaimed are engaging in the serious and detailed critique to which Christianity must be subjected. Feminist voices within this work are essential. Their absence is a detriment to women and to the whole Christian tradition. Christianity is in fact guilty of perpetuating the second-class status of women and enabling their subjugation and abuse. After finding it guilty, feminists need to hold Christianity accountable for changing, thereby stopping its patriarchal deeds.

Christianity is guilty of misunderstanding women, holding them back, and legitimating their abuse, so feminists must subject it to scrutiny and hold it accountable for failure or for renewal.

SUGGESTED READING

Carole R. Bohn. "Dominion to Rule: The Roots and Consequences of a Theology of Ownership." 1989.

Elizabeth A. Clark and Herbert Richardson. "Woman as Witch." 1996.

Christine Gudorf. "Contraception and Abortion in Roman Catholicism." 2000.

Rosemary Radford Ruether, editor. *Religion and Sexism: Images of Woman in the Jewish and Christian Traditions.* 1974.

1.3 HAS CHRISTIANITY BEEN OPPRESSIVE ONLY ON THE BASIS OF GENDER?

One of the more shameful legacies of the Christian tradition has been its use as the ideological basis for the persecution of

Jews and Muslims. In addition, Christianity has provided religious justification for the careless misuse of the earth's natural resources. Each of these realities is taken seriously by third-wave feminists, who are attuned not only to oppression on the basis of gender but also to justice throughout the global and multifaith human community. Looking at examples of how Christianity has been oppressive in other ways also reveals how initiatives to correct these problems have emerged.

The Holocaust was in part made possible by centuries of Christian anti-Semitism, itself a gross misconstrual of the religion's relationship to Judaism. At the heart of the matter is the very difficult question of whether Christianity is inherently anti-Jewish because of its supersessionist tendencies. Supersessionism is the belief that Christianity supersedes, completes, and fulfills Judaism. It is the belief that once Christianity arrived, Judaism was no longer needed because Jesus was the messiah, the promised deliverer of the Jews; and anyone who didn't understand that was simply wrong. Since the beginning, Christians have had to walk a very fine line by maintaining a connection to Judaism while adhering to their claims that Jesus is God incarnate. Early Christianity was full of unfortunate tendencies to belittle Jews for their supposed ignorance because they did not accept Jesus as their savior. In Romans, for example, Paul speaks directly about the Jews when he says, "I can testify that they have a zeal for God, but it is not enlightened" (Romans 10:2).

Such problematic views did not end with the early centuries. In fact, they were in some ways solidified and entrenched. In 1543, Martin Luther wrote "On the Jews and Their Lies," which reflected his own move from a theological anti-Judaism to a racist anti-Semitism. For among other things, he lambasted the Jews for refusing to accept Jesus as their savior (a theological point) and called them a lazy and irrational people (a racist point).[4]

The Nazis in Germany were the fullest and most complex expression of a long history of anti-Semitism. The Christian churches in Europe retain a shameful legacy of nonintervention and collaboration in the mistreatment and murder of millions of Jews.[5] The weight of history clearly indicts Christianity for failing its Jewish neighbors, but glimmers of hope for a better future have since emerged. The World Council of Churches (WCC), founded in 1948 in part as a reaction to world's collective failure in the Holocaust, holds as one of its chief purposes to "engage in Christian service by serving human need, breaking down barriers between people, seeking justice and peace."[6] Seminars on human rights, religions of the world, and interfaith community building are now regularly offered at the WCC ecumenical institute at Bossey in Switzerland. In addition, the Second Vatican Council of the Roman Catholic Church in the 1960s held discussions and produced official documents that took seriously the need for the Church to repair its relationship with Judaism. *Nostra Aetate* spoke of the "spiritual patrimony common to Christians and Jews" and rejected "any discrimination against men or harassment of them because of their race, color, condition of life, or religion."[7] These are just a few examples of the ways that Christianity

---

4. Luther, "On the Jews and Their Lies," 123–306.

5. Barnett, "The Role of the Churches," 55–58.

6. World Council of Churches, "Who Are We?" para. 4.

7. Second Vatican Council, *Declaration on the Relationship of the Church to Non-Christian Religions* (*Nostra Aetate*)," 660–68.

has addressed the problems of its tenuous relationship with Judaism throughout history.

Christianity's relationship with Islam has a similarly violent and troubled past. The early twentieth-century *Catholic Encyclopedia* described the Crusades as "expeditions undertaken, in fulfillment of a solemn vow, to deliver the Holy Places from Mohammedan tyranny."[8] Christian beliefs here gave way to violent interaction with nations and people of other faiths. Various church-sanctioned military expeditions during the eleventh, twelfth, and thirteenth centuries resulted in shifting political boundaries and widespread resentment against Christianity. In addition, "viewed from the aspect of their purposes the Crusades were failures. They made no permanent conquest of the Holy Land . . . Their cost in lives and treasure was enormous. Though initiated in a high spirit of devotion, their conduct was disgraced throughout by quarrels, divided motives, and low standards of personal conduct."[9]

The impetus for this action was at least in part a misunderstanding of the religion of Islam, reflected by Christians' not only misnaming it with terms like "Mohammedan" but also believing it to be inherently tyrannical. These misunderstandings along with the history of aggressive colonialism working to ensure Christian domination of the world inform an increasingly complex relationship between the Christian-dominated West and the Islamic-defined Middle East, well into the twentieth and twenty-first centuries.

Today much of Christianity better understands its familial relationship with both Judaism and Islam, and faithful

8. Bréhier, "Crusades," para. 1.

9. Walker, *A History of the Christian Church*, 224.

scholars and leaders have worked to outline the necessity for and consequences of cooperation among the religions and their adherents. The National Council of Churches in the U.S. strengthens interfaith relations through various events and projects, and the Council on American-Islamic Relations today has ongoing interfaith outreach with Christian churches and their members. All this work is even more crucial in a world where *Muslim* is too often wrongly associated with *terrorist*, and the civil rights of Muslims in the U.S. have been under constant threat since the terrorist attacks of September 11, 2001.[10] Islamic feminist movements have also emerged in this context, taking seriously women's experiences both within their religion and as citizens of countries ravaged by sectarian violence and international military occupation. Third-wave feminism needs to engage these issues in order to fully participate in movements for peace and justice around the world.

A final example takes seriously the Christian theological justification for human misuse of the earth. Often because of an interpretation of Genesis 1:28 that exhorts humans to subdue the earth, the Christian tradition has viewed humans as the most important part of creation. Along with that, the rest of the earth is secondary and subjected completely to the whims and wishes of human beings. The consequences of viewing humans as masters of the universe was famously connected to Christianity by Lynn White Jr. in his 1967 article, "The Historical Roots of Our Ecologic Crisis" in the

10. The CAIR produces annual reports as well as periodic statements on legal issues, public opinion, and issues relevant to Muslims in America: http://www.cair.com/AmericanMuslims/ReportsandSurveys .aspx/.

magazine *Science.* In response to environmental awareness and activism that emerged over the past two generations, Christian churches, groups, and leaders are moving to articulate the trusteeship of creation that is given to humans by God. Leading second-wave feminist theologian Rosemary Radford Ruether has written "an ecofeminist theology of earth healing" that draws together resources from the Christian tradition to identify both its contributions to the destruction of the planet and the resources it provides for healing the earth.

Third-wave feminists can see how, with regard to Jews, Muslims, and the earth, Christianity has been oppressive in a variety of ways. Feminism is a key critical voices that raises questions about power dynamics, about privilege and oppression in relationships with others, and about environmental exploitation. This is because patriarchy depends on and feeds off of racism, classism, and heterosexism as well as global capitalism, environmental racism, and religious discrimination. Third-wave feminism is keenly interested in the global reality of human life, which includes a multifaith community as well as responsibility for the effects of human participation in the ecosystem. If Christianity is not held to higher standards of relating to outsiders, insiders, and the planet, it will continue to support the destruction and division brought about by patriarchy.

Feminists can also recognize faithful activism and movement for change in things like the World Council of Churches and its national counterpart, as well as various denominational efforts on a number of issues like interfaith dialogue and ecological justice. Working with Christians who also recognize the pernicious problems of violence and exploitation, feminists can eradicate more suffering and construct a more viable human community in the twenty-first century.

The shameful Christian legacy of violence and exploitation of other religious people and the earth is being overcome by faithful activism in which feminists can and should participate.

SUGGESTED READING

Leila Ahmed. *Women and Gender in Islam: Historical Roots of a Modern Debate.* 1993.

The Harvard Pluralism Project. *Women's Networks Initiatives.* Online: http://www.pluralism.org/women/.

Carol Rittner, et al., editors. *The Holocaust and the Christian World: Reflections on the Past, Challenges for the Future.* 2000.

Rosemary Radford Ruether. *Gaia & God: An Ecofeminist Theology of Earth Healing.* 1992.

1.4 HOW HAS CHRISTIANITY AFFECTED WOMEN'S LIVES IN A POSITIVE WAY?

Christianity has provided both a set of beliefs and a place that have been good for women individually and collectively. While the oppressive and sexist tendencies of the religion are well documented and discussed, its empowering dimension is often overlooked by feminist critics. History, theology, and practice are instructive on this topic. Historically, Christians created a community that welcomed the marginalized and served the poor, and this practice can be found resurging today. Theologically, Christianity provides a basis for egalitarian and just human relationships. In practice, Christian churches have been and still are places where women have found and fostered community, developed leadership skills, and transformed the societies in which they live.

The early Christian community was viewed by the dominant class as a radical and threatening sect because of its claims about Jesus, and because it welcomed women, slaves, and members of the lower social classes. Based in part on stories of Jesus' speaking to women in public (John 4), women's presence throughout his ministry (Luke 8), and his compassion for marginalized people (Matthew 9:10–12), the Christian community was founded on the belief in a compassionate God who demonstrated on many occasions compassionate care for the poor and oppressed. In this way, early Christians continued the narrative that originated with the Israelite people's belief in God as the one who liberated the Israelites from slavery in Egypt, and who sustained them while exiled in Babylon.

In response to the worsening conditions of daily life for multitudes of people throughout Latin America, this belief in a God who opts for the poor and marginalized was revitalized as a core principle of Christianity in 1968. Inspired by the Second Vatican Council, Latin American bishops gathered at Medellín, Colombia, for a conference, and Gustavo Gutiérrez emerged as a leading voice of what became liberation theology. Gutiérrez and the liberation movement insisted that Christianity was a religion that had become excessively focused on the afterlife and needed to become a religion more focused on the quality of life this world: "When we struggle for a just world in which there is not servitude, oppression, or slavery, we are signifying the coming of the messiah."[11]

11. Gutiérrez, "Toward a Theology of Liberation," 73.

This opened up and affirmed entirely new forms of activism devoted to economic and social justice around the world. What liberation theology did was "shift the gaze" (to borrow Gutiérrez's phrase) of Christianity toward more careful attention to the injustices in human life here and now. This included justice for women.

The positive theological legacy of Christianity can be seen in the women scholars it has produced and the ordinary women who struggle for justice in their daily lives as well as in their church. Some of the most prominent feminist theologians of the second wave have been women raised and educated in the Roman Catholic tradition; this demonstrates that the same tradition that limits women's access to leadership provides them with the intellectual and spiritual tools to challenge and change the tradition. Rosemary Radford Ruether, Mary Daly, Elizabeth Johnson, and Ada María Isasi-Díaz are all women whose theological criticism has sustained a practical movement for equality and justice for women. When feminist scholars unmask sexism in biblical interpretation, church history, and theological ideas, they are contributing to a reform of Christianity that benefits everyone.

This contemporary reform of Christianity has been possible because of the vision of human equality and dignity inherent in its theologies. It has been possible because of the core belief in a God who liberates and who opts for those whom society shuns. Throughout church history, women's struggles with and against ecclesial structures have produced a collection of work that continues to reform a tradition and to inspire a new generation of Christian theologians.

Practically speaking, Christian churches have been hubs of ordinary women's leadership, sometimes in spite of official denominational pronouncements to the contrary. Cheryl Townsend Gilkes's descriptive book title articulates a reality that many people know to be true: *If It Wasn't For the Women*. Gilkes takes this phrase from a conversation she had with a bookstore manager who declared: "If it wasn't for the women, you wouldn't have a church!"[12] Many women social activists throughout history have taken their cue from their Christian identity. This is not only a modern phenomenon, as some medieval women's writing demonstrates. Catherine of Siena spoke out when she wrote to Pope Gregory XI in 1376 about the corrupt state of the church, urging the return of the papacy to Rome as well as the reform of its excessive focus on worldly things. Despite official limits on women's leadership in Christianity, women have a long history of finding ways to change their communities and their church.

In American history, women who headed up the anti-lynching movement and the temperance and prohibition movements honed their organizational and leadership skills in their churches. In a society where women were not permitted to hold elective office, to vote, or to own property in their own names, Christian churches were places where women designed, implemented, and led programs and projects in their local communities. Ida B. Wells-Barnett wrote, spoke, and organized protests against lynching in the late nineteenth century. Another female social activist at the time, with whom Barnett publically sparred, was Frances Willard, president of the Women's Christian Temperance Union. There are many examples of social change led by women who gained practical leadership skills in their Christian churches, and who took

12. Gilkes, *If It Wasn't for the Women*, 1.

many of their ideological commitments to community service, compassion, justice, and peace from that tradition.

Insofar as Christianity has contributed to many different social movements for justice and equality, it has been good for women. The Christian connections of the civil rights movement in the 1960s are well known, with Rev. Dr. Martin Luther King Jr. at the helm of the Southern Christian Leadership Conference. It is true that the sexist tendencies of that and other organizations in the civil-rights and black-power eras have since been unmasked by scholars and activists. The Southern Poverty Law Center's "Teaching Tolerance" curriculum specifically includes tools for discussing and responding to sexism in the life and work of otherwise lionized heroes like Dr. King.[13] Despite this reality, such movements were specifically good for women of color in their challenge to racism and their contribution to achievements like outlawing segregation through the *Brown v. Board of Education* Supreme Court decision in 1954 and ensuring black citizens' equal access to the vote through the Voting Rights Act of 1965. Third-wave feminism is keenly interested in the intersection of problems like racism and sexism. Recognizing the ways in which Christianity was a foundational piece of these movements contributes to a fuller understanding of them.

Christianity has influenced women's lives in a positive way in spite of the many ways that it has limited and denigrated them. This is a testament both to the power of the religion and to the power of the women within it to make their lives and their world better. Women have consistently found ways to survive, thrive, and improve every community and

13. Holladay, "Sexism in the Civil Rights Movement."

institution of which they have been a part. Christianity is one of those institutions, providing theological and practical tools that have been and can be used by women for positive social and personal change.

Christianity has been good for women because of its theological vision of equality under a compassionate God, and because of its historical and present practice of radical community organizing and transformation led by women.'

Suggested Reading

Cheryl Townsend Gilkes. *If It Wasn't for the Women: Black Women's Experience and Womanist Culture in Church and Community.* 2001.

Gustavo Gutiérrez, "Toward a Theology of Liberation." 1968.

Mary Catherine Hilkert. *Speaking with Authority: Catherine of Siena and the Voices of Women Today.* 2008.

Rosemary Radford Ruether and Rosemary Skinner Keller, general editors. *Women and Religion in America.* 2 vols. 1981 and 1983.

Emilie Townes. *Womanist Justice, Womanist Hope.* 1993.

1.5 How Are Feminists Changing the Fact That Christianity Has Been Anti-feminist, If Not Anti-woman?

Feminists have been changing the sexist and misogynist tendencies of Christianity for generations. Examples from the first wave, the second wave, and the third wave of feminism demonstrate clearly how Christianity is in places becoming a pro-feminist and pro-woman religion. Continuing these efforts now is essential for the well-being of women and men around the world.

In the modern world, significant attempts to critically engage the Christian tradition gained public attention with the writings of abolitionist women and suffragists like Sarah Grimke, Elizabeth Cady Stanton, and Matilda Joslyn Gage. Grimke wrote *Letters on the Equality of the Sexes* in 1838, and in these letters she criticized sexist interpretations of a variety of biblical texts in order to make her case for the equality of men and women. She modestly pointed out one of the disadvantages to women, saying, "When we are admitted to the honor of studying Greek and Hebrew, we shall produce some various readings of the Bible a little different from those we have now." And despite her lack of advanced education, she was able to recognize that Jesus put forth ideas for all to follow "without any reference to sex or condition."[14]

Stanton's and Gage's efforts to construct *The Woman's Bible* appeared in two volumes in 1895 and 1898, representing another significant shot at patriarchally dominated schools of biblical interpretation. The effort itself, while not wholly successful, was monumental in scope, especially in its context. The legacy of *The Woman's Bible* is mixed because of the anti-Semitism present throughout, and the less-than-professional methodology used when Stanton physically cut out passages from the Bible. Because of several factors, it was not substantial enough to have a lasting impression on the field of biblical studies. Stanton and Gage were not trained scholars in the field of biblical commentary (a nineteenth-century woman rarely was, as Grimke had pointed out) and therefore were not able to break through. Gage went on to write a text with

14. Grimke, "Letters on the Equality of the Sexes," 242.

greater impact called *Woman, Church, and State* in 1893, in which she laid out the many ways the church has contributed to maintaining sexism and women's second-class citizenship. The strategies these nineteenth century women employed reflect their key insight that getting to the heart of religious justifications for sexism must be part of combating it.

Two important feminist theological works in the second-wave feminism were more substantial in their impact and marked an irrevocable shift in Christian theology. Valerie Saiving's article called "The Human Situation," published in the *Journal of Religion* in 1960, directly addressed the flaws in theological giant Reinhold Neibuhr's discussions of human nature and sin. Saiving showed how Niebuhr's focus on pride as the central human sin was steeped in androcentric thinking and did not resonate with women's experiences. On the contrary, Saiving argued, women suffer from socially conditioned passivity. Their sin is, in fact, too little pride and not enough self-assertion. She pointed out that Christian exhortations for the faithful to humble themselves do not take into account those whom Christianity already humiliates. She showed definitively how Christian theology provided divine justification for the social reality of sexism and the second-class status of women. Saiving's argument influenced not only the specific field of Christian theological anthropology which discusses sin in particular, but also the entire Christian tradition which had up to that point been able to think and act based solely on male human experience.

A concurrent social development inspired by second-wave feminism was the emerging understanding in the medical sciences that testing and research on any number of diseases and conditions could no longer be done solely with male subjects. A conference on women's health and women's bodies in 1969 led to the formation of the Boston Women's Health Collective, and the publication of the groundbreaking book *Our Bodies, Ourselves* in 1971. Thus, activists in theology and in the sciences reached these conclusions about expanding their understanding of "human" experience around the same time because of second-wave feminism. No research on the human condition, spiritually or biologically, could be done in the same way after these breakthroughs in understanding "human" experience.

Another second-wave feminist theologian, Mary Daly, influenced the Christian tradition of thinking and speaking about God. In 1973 Daly encapsulated the problem of male images of God, about which she had been speaking and writing for many years. Drawing the connection between theology and sociology, Daly stated that "if God is male, then the male is god."[15] She showed how theological ideas have sociological roots as well as consequences. In fact, using theories of religion from Peter Berger and others, Daly showed that a group ascribes to its deity the attributes that it finds to be the highest and the most ideal. In patriarchy, that is first and foremost the male. Christian theology that has taken place after Mary Daly, whether it agrees with her or not, has had to reckon with the undeniable implications of exclusively male images and language for God.

Many theologians have picked up precisely on that challenge and have constructed feminist liturgies as well as participating in reshaping cross-denominational worship resources. The Inclusive Language Lectionary project in 1983 represented the National Council of Churches' belief that "All persons are equally loved, judged, and accepted by God . . . God is more

15. Daly, *Beyond God the Father*, 19.

than male or female, and is more than can be described in historically and culturally limiting terms."[16] This is one example of putting into practice the theological claim made by Daly and others that exclusive male imagery and language for God is problematic. It also shows how Christian theologians, feminist or not, understand the problem of sexism. At the same time, the New Revised Standard Version of the Bible (NRSV), which was completed in 1989, openly addressed "the danger of linguistic sexism arising from the inherent bias of the English language toward the masculine gender, a bias that in the case of the Bible has often restricted or obscured the meaning of the original text."[17] These two pan-Christian efforts in particular show how feminists and supporters of anti-sexism work have been directly changing the fact that Christianity has been anti-woman and anti-feminist.

Feminist theology in the third wave is more complex and continues to unfold around us today. Reflecting the third wave's intersectional focus on race, class, gender, sexuality, and ecology among other things, the later ecofeminist work of Rosemary Radford Ruether, the work of womanist theologian Delores S. Williams, and the thinking of mujerista theologian Ada María Isasi-Díaz set the stage for the more diffuse and complex relationship between feminism and Christianity with which we now live. Ruether's 1992 book *Gaia and God* spells out the responsibilities of Christianity to move toward a more ecologically minded theology; Williams, along with scholars like Jacquelyn Grant, inspired a generation of black (i.e. womanist) activists to engage the Christian tradition from their particular "tridimensional" experience at

16. Gold, *An Inclusive Language Lectionary*, 1.
17. Attridge, "To the Reader," in *The HarperCollins Study Bible*, xxiii.

the intersection of race, class, and gender; Isasi-Díaz recenters Christian theology and ethics on the struggles that define Hispanic women's lives, recasting moral agency *en la lucha* (in the struggle).

While the battles for the ordination and equality of women in Christian churches defined much of the second wave, struggles for gay and lesbian Christians for full access to legal rights and church practices like marriage and ordination have begun to characterize one way that the third wave of feminism continues to change Christianity. Daniel Helminiak's basic text, *What the Bible Really Says about Homosexuality*, as well as the work of Episcopal bishop John Shelby Spong and church activists like Lutheran pastor Anita C. Hill continue to reframe Christian understandings of inclusion and social justice.

As third-wave feminists continue to challenge the multifaceted sexism of Christianity, they are moving their attention to the global religious context. Attending to the reality of women's lives around the world becomes more important as Christianity grows in Latin America and Africa, and as the world understands more thoroughly than ever before the multireligious nature of the global community. These are the ways that third-wave feminist activism is moving its own advocacy work firmly into the new millennium, and the ways that it needs to continue to reform Christianity for a new generation.

Feminists are changing the fact that Christianity has been anti-feminist and anti-woman through activism, scholarly engagement, and faithful participation that has already resulted in denominational and biblical shifts toward inclusion.

Suggested Reading

Mary Daly. *Beyond God the Father*. 1973.

Matilda Joslyn Gage. *Woman, Church and State*. (1893) 2002.

Jacquelyn Grant. *White Women's Christ and Black Women's Jesus*. 1989.

Ada María Isasi-Díaz. *En la Lucha = In the Struggle: Elaborating a Mujerista Theology; A Hispanic Women's Liberation Theology*. 1993.

Valerie Saiving Goldstein. "The Human Situation: A Feminine View." 1960.

1.6 If Jesus Was a Feminist, and Paul Was a Misogynist, What's the Real Christianity?

In some efforts to demonstrate the compatibility of feminism with Christianity, two tendencies often emerge: painting Jesus as an anti-patriarchal protofeminist who really wanted to advance the rights of women, and conversely painting Paul as an irrevocable misogynist who corrupted an otherwise peaceful, woman-friendly religion. Neither of those carica-tures is completely true. What is true requires a slightly more in-depth examination of the factors that sometimes lead to these broad statements: Jesus did challenge the patriarchal power structure of his time, and Paul's letters do contain some of the more misogynist texts of the New Testament. But neither one's legacy for Christianity is limited to that.

   First, it is important to state that calling Jesus a feminist is entirely anachronistic: it is a concept and a word that was not in existence during his life, and it implies a set of principles that cannot be fairly applied to him. However, the underlying claim that Jesus supported the equal humanity of women is one that can be explored by examining the texts and stories that have been preserved. Elisabeth Schüssler Fiorenza discusses at length some of the other potential problems with highlighting Jesus' liberating effect for women, including an anti-Judaism tendency that arises in Christianity. Such a view falsely claims that Judaism was (and by implication still is) oppressive for women, but then Jesus came along and freed everyone.

Opposing this view, first in her book *In Memory of Her* (1983), and later in *Jesus: Miriam's Child, Sophia's Prophet* (1994), Schüssler Fiorenza discusses the Jesus movement as one of several Jewish movements of the first century, and one that in fact was pro-women. Jesus and his followers were Jewish, and by most accounts they understood his ministry and their work to be taking place within a tradition to which they continued to be faithful. Throughout the gospels, numerous examples of women's presence and significance exist: They were participants in his ministry (Matthew 15:21; 26:6), were present for his death on the cross (Mark 15:40), and were the first witnesses to the resurrection in all four canonical gospels (Mark 16; Matthew 28; Luke 24; John 20). In addition, we read in the upper-room scene in Acts that the eleven were there "together with certain women, including Mary the mother of Jesus" (Acts 1:14). These examples are of a community that in many ways acted counter to conventional wisdom about interactions between unrelated men and women in the ancient world. The New Testament does in fact show Jesus as a man who respected, communicated with, and fully engaged women in his preaching about the kingdom of God; but by no means ought any first-century man be regarded as feminist.

The Pauline letters are a slightly more complicated set of texts that require some basic familiarity with the historical-critical study of the Bible to understand. New Testament scholars generally agree that Paul was actually the author of seven of the letters in the Bible today: First Thessalonians, Philippians, Philemon, Galatians, First and Second Corinthians, and Romans. This means that the authorship of six of the Pauline letters is at least in dispute: Second Thessalonians, Colossians, Ephesians, First and Second Timothy, and Titus. Plenty of Christians believe that Paul is indisputably the author of all thirteen letters, but the majority of Bible scholars agree that there are historical and stylistic reasons to doubt the authenticity of the latter, what are often called deutero-pauline, letters.

In addition to the complicated task of sorting out the authorship of the letters themselves, within letters there are passages nearly impossible to translate, and other passages widely believed to be added by later editors or scribes as the texts were copied and passed on to other communities. One example of this is 1 Corinthians 11:10, where Paul is discussing proper behavior in public worship and states that women need to have their heads covered. The text reads "a woman ought to have a symbol of authority on her head, because of the angels." One translation note, a footnote in the *HarperCollins Study Bible* (NRSV) indicates bluntly that "There is no scholarly consensus about the translation of this verse."[18] This verse occurs in a larger passage often used to justify female subordination to males because Paul is here asserting that women have to have something or someone in charge of them. Questions about its actual meaning, therefore,

18. Attridge, *HarperCollins Study Bible*, 1946 (1 Cor 11:10n).

have significant implications for feminists and Christians trying to understand these passages and their influence.

Another example in the same letter is 1 Corinthians
14:33b–36, where Paul says that "women should be silent in
the churches. For they are not permitted to speak, but should
be subordinate, as the law also says." This text is so much in
dispute that in several translations and editions of the Bible
it is placed in parentheses or brackets, and the *HarperCollins
Study Bible* (NRSV) note reads as follows: "Some interpreters
regard the instruction for women to be silent in churches as
a later, non-Pauline addition to the Letter, more in keeping
with the viewpoint of the Pastoral Letters than of the certainly
Pauline Letters."[19] Those Pastoral Letters include Ephesians
and 1 and 2 Timothy, where a clear model of female subordination is promoted, inconsistent with the indisputably
Pauline letters, which speak frequently of women's leadership
in Paul's own ministry as well as in the communities he established. The suggestion scholars make about 1 Corinthians 14
is that one of the later authors, as he was editing or copying
Paul's text inserted this passage to confirm and legitimate the
later author's own view. Other interpreters suggest that even if
the words were from Paul himself, they were likely related to
the specific situation at the time in Corinth; "women keep si-
lence" is just one in a sequence to specific kinds of disruptions
in the worship at Corinth (and the specificity of the context is
important): tongue-speaking without an interpreter (14:28),
multiple prophetic speakers (14:30), and women asking questions in the worship service (14:34).

The ultimate question feminists may have is whether or
not the authenticity and actual meaning of these texts matters,

19. Ibid., 1952 (1 Corinthians 14:35–36n).

when they have clearly been used by a religion that worked hard to ensure the second-class status of women. Understanding the possibilities for varied authorship is important because generations of faith communities put so much weight on texts like these. When feminists are equipped with more detailed knowledge of these texts and their history, they are able to more effectively critique the arguments that rest on their supposed subordination of women.

The worldview of Paul is also an important factor in understanding what he was and was not focusing on. Paul, like a lot of first-century Christians, believed sincerely in the imminent return of Christ. The belief that the end was near and that the Savior was to be expected at any moment led to practices like avoiding marriage and children (1 Corinthians 7). Many important events and trends—including the destruction of the temple in Jerusalem in the year 70 and the dominance of the growing Roman empire—led early Christians to believe that they were living through the final cosmic battle of good and evil. Apocalyptic literature like the book of Revelation reflects this worldview. Because of this, concern for justice issues—like the social equality of all people—were not at all in the forefront of early Christianity. When Paul proclaimed in Galatians 3:28 that "there is no longer Jew or Greek, there is no longer slave or free, there is no longer male and female," he was not actually trying to establish the ideal egalitarian community here on earth. He was emphasizing the final phrase of the same verse: "for all of you are one in Christ Jesus." He cared completely about inclusive membership in the group and the spiritual reality of the afterlife.

As noted, a larger question in both cases here is whether it matters what Jesus actually said and did with regard to women, and what Paul actually wrote and did with regard to women. Perhaps what matters even more is understanding the centuries of interpretation of these texts, during which major interpreters almost always opted for the more sexist reading. Understanding texts and their ancient context does matter when adherents of Christianity claim to base their actions on them. When so much weight is put on ancient authors and leaders, deeper knowledge about them is crucial for believers and scholars as well as feminist critics.

Based just on these two figures, it is clear that discerning "the real" Christianity is as impossible a task as there ever was. According to whom? Based on what details? Since the rise of historical scholarship in the eighteenth and nineteenth centuries and the subsequent flourishing of things like biblical archaeology, people have wrestled with the question of what Jesus actually said, what Paul actually wrote, and, more important, of what difference it makes. With regard to questions about women and social justice, Christians must contend as much with the traditions of interpretation as they must contend with the foundational texts themselves. Learning more about Jesus and Paul is only part of the story.

While it is anachronistic to claim that Jesus was a feminist, and too limiting to name Paul a misogynist, deeper knowledge about each of the historical figures is simply part of the larger story of Christianity.

SUGGESTED READING

Stanley Grenz with Denise Kjesbo. *Women in the Church.* 1995.

Sandra Hack Polaski. *A Feminist Introduction to Paul.* 2005.

Elisabeth Schüssler Fiorenza. *Jesus: Miriam's Child, Sophia's Prophet.* 1995.

1.7 How Do Different Christian Sects or Denominations Deal with Women?

Christianity has always been a diverse religion and currently is composed of groups that exclude women from major leadership positions as well as of those that completely affirm women in leadership. This spectrum of allowing women in leadership or not corresponds roughly with beliefs and theologies that range from viewing women as subservient, if not as second-class citizens, to those that are completely egalitarian in their understanding women and men both as equally human, imbued with the same human dignity and rights. A few select examples are included here, to represent the range of issues and positions in Christianity of specific interest to feminists.

The largest and most influential Christian tradition that excludes women from leadership positions and continues to adhere to strict patriarchal prescriptions for gender roles is the Roman Catholic Church. Women are officially prohibited from entering the priesthood and are exhorted to fulfill their God-given role to be mothers and wives. The continued total ban on contraception reveals the church's position on what women can and should do. Some examples from papal documents more specifically reveal Catholic teaching on women's roles. In 1930, Pope Pius XI issued *Casti Connubii* (*On Christian Marriage*), perhaps not coincidentally just a decade after first-wave feminist activism resulted in women attaining the right to vote in the United States. The encyclical letter clearly has this in mind when it discusses "false teachers" who assert the dangerous idea "that the rights of husband and wife are equal" as well as the supposed emancipation that the false teachers are promoting. On the contrary, the letter proclaims that those social, economic, and physiological dimensions are a "false liberty and unnatural equality with the husband [which] is to the detriment of the woman herself . . ."[20] This early twentieth-century document reflects one moment when the church was reacting to social and economic changes taking place in the world, and strongly speaking against movements for freedom and equality for women.

The late twentieth century brought similar Church reactions to and rejections of shifting social conditions. In 1968, *Humanae Vitae* (*On the Regulation of Birth*) was issued by Pope Paul VI to address questions about procreation and contraception, responding to the recommendations of a commission set up by Pope John XXIII in 1963 to address such questions. The timing of this letter is eight years after the FDA approved oral contraception, and in the middle of the 1960s civil rights movements. The encyclical letter makes clear in paragraph 6 that the conclusions of the commission (to relax the absolute ban on the use of contraception) were actually *not* going to be adopted by the Church. In paragraph 14, the Church's position that contraception is "to be absolutely excluded" is reasserted, contrary to the commission and over against the 1951 statements of Pope Pius XII that the so-called rhythm method (planning intercourse around a woman's fertile times) be allowed.

These two documents correspond with the first and second waves of feminism, showcasing the Church's reactions to it. On May 30, 2008, well into the present third wave of feminism, Pope Benedict XVI's Congregation for the Doctrine of the Faith proclaimed on the front page of the Vatican's weekly newspaper that any Catholic bishop found to be irregularly

20. Vatican, "*Casti Connubii* (On Christian Marriage)," §§74–75.

ordaining women will be excommunicated, along with the woman herself.[21] The statement was issued, in part, in response to "irregular" ordinations of women that had been taking place around the world for several years: the Danube Seven in Germany in 2002; nine women in Ontario, Canada, in 2005; two women in Minneapolis in 2007; and four women in Chicago in 2008.[22]

A relatively influential Christian tradition in the United States that excludes women from leadership and encourages their submission to husbands is the Southern Baptist Convention (SBC). The case of the Southern Baptists is somewhat more complicated by their unique ecclesial structure, where the national church body has historically had no direct power to dictate the practices of independent local congregations. For that reason, there are some women pastors in the Southern Baptist tradition. Since 1979, however, the SBC has been on a decidedly conservative trajectory. More fundamentalist and conservative members of the denomination gained control over all the church boards through various elections in the 1980s, thus altering the culture and expectations for congregations.[23] This shift of the tradition culminated in "The Baptist Faith & Message" statement adopted in 2000, which states among other things that "the office of pastor is limited to men as qualified by Scripture."[24] At that point, Southern Baptists joined other, smaller Christian denominations in the

21. Wooden, "Attempts to Ordain Women," par. 1.

22. Information on these events and other activism relating to women's ordination in the Catholic Church can be found at http://www.womensordination.org

23. Schmidt, *A Still Small Voice*, 101-127.

24. Southern Baptist Convention, "The Baptist Faith & Message," sec. 6, par. 1.

category of excluding women from full participation in leadership positions: the Lutheran Church–Missouri Synod, the Christian Reformed Church, and the Church of Jesus Christ of Latter-day Saints, among others.

Somewhat in the middle of the political and theological spectrum are mainline Christian denominations like the Episcopal Church, the Evangelical Lutheran Church in America (ELCA), the United Methodist Church (UMC) and the Presbyterian Church USA (PCUSA). These are denominations that began ordaining women in the 1960s and 1970s, that now have public statements on contraception and abortion preserving family's rights to faithfully make their own decisions, and that are presently in various stages of struggling with the inclusion into all facets of church life and leadership of those who are gay and lesbian. The Episcopal Church has been in conflict with the worldwide Anglican Communion over its shifts toward inclusion of gays and lesbians in higher-level positions. The ELCA has wrestled with its questions around sexuality through various task forces and churchwide studies over the past decade. In August 2009, the church wide assembly voted to affirm monogamous committed same-gender relationships, and to allow individuals in those relationships to be candidates for ministry.

At the inclusive end of the spectrum, where the longest and fullest traditions of inclusion can be found (both on women's leadership as well as in theological positions) are denominations such as the Unitarian Universalist Church, the United Church of Christ (UCC), and Quakers. Such Christian traditions have been small but significant in producing women leaders as far back as during the nineteenth-century battles against slavery and in organizing for women's right to vote. The UCC and its predecessor church bodies emphasize freedom of religious expression, local church independence, and diversity. They also have the honor of ordaining the first woman in modern Christian history, with the Congregationalist Church leader Antoinette Brown in New York in 1853. Today the UCC actively welcomes and ordains gays and lesbians when other Christian churches refuse to do so. Delegates declared it a "Just Peace Church" in 1985, and the denomination has a record of politically liberal positions on issues including economic justice, peace activism, and gender equality.

Upon reviewing such a wide range of ideas and practices with regard to women by traditions that are all a part of Christianity, feminists might be tempted to weigh them all out in order to make an overall judgment about the relative merits of Christianity when it comes to women. It is likely that Christianity would not come out favorably in such a measurement. The weight of history brings too much sexism and misogyny to the scales and continues to be a factor holding Christianity back.

What is more interesting and perhaps more meaningful, however, is the direction in which the religion can be said to be moving. Despite passionate threats of excommunication and public assertions of male power from the Vatican and Southern Baptist leaders, the tradition of Christianity has been on an inclusive and justice-oriented track for several generations. It moves slower than some other social institutions, and often steps backward. But merely examining the position of women in Christian denominations and the statements about women by Christian denominations in 1900 against the same denominations in 2000 reveals a movement toward inclusion. The resistance efforts are fierce. A growing conservative evangelical form of Christianity has paralleled these movements for inclusion and diversity, working against everything from scientific literacy to equal rights for women. Despite these loud cries of opposition, the fact remains that Christianity has a bent toward justice that prevails over time and overall.

Different Christian denominations deal with women in a variety of ways, from complete exclusion to complete inclusion in leadership roles; a corresponding diversity of ideas about women's equality and humanity reveals that despite a bent toward justice, sectors of the religion continue to have loud and powerful leaders working hard to preserve patriarchal power.

SUGGESTED READING

Because the positions of churches are often undergoing reform, I encourage the consultation of any denomination's official Web site for historical documents, position statements, and ongoing discussions. These are just a few that have been mentioned:

Episcopal Church, USA: http://ecusa.anglican.org/

Evangelical Lutheran Church in America: http://www.elca.org/

Presbyterian Church (USA): http://www.pcusa.org/

Roman Catholic Church: http://www.vatican.va/

Southern Baptist Convention: http://www.sbc.net/

United Church of Christ: http://www.ucc.org/

1.8 Is Christianity Better or Worse for Women Than Other Religions?

Feminists are rightly tempted to classify all religions as irredeemably patriarchal. It is more correct and more complicated to understand that the overarching problem is patriarchy. Religion has been one of the many institutions that patriarchy uses as a tool to justify and maintain the beliefs and practices that subordinate women. Because of that, most religions that exist in the contemporary world are those that have survived under global patriarchy: They are religions that support or have posed little threat to patriarchy. Looking more closely, examples from the other two Abrahamic traditions as well as some Eastern religions show that every religion has its own strengths and inherent limitations when it comes to a liberating life for women and men.

Christianity, Judaism, and Islam trace their roots back to the patriarch Abraham and the stories of his wives and sons recorded in Genesis and in the Quran. These three religions therefore share some foundations, but historically they created and maintained different cultures as well as theologies. Like Christianity, Judaism throughout history and today is a diverse religion with varying traditions within it. Reform Judaism allows for the ordination of women as rabbis, while Orthodox Judaism does not and places strict limitations on the public interactions of men and women. Reconstructionist Jews present alternate interpretations of Leviticus's injunctions against male-male sex, while in March 2007 the Jewish Theological Seminary, the premiere educational institution in Conservative Judaism, announced that it was accepting qualified gay and lesbian students after a long process of discernment regarding the halakhic status of homosexuality.[25]

Jewish feminists such as Judith Plaskow and Susannah Heschel have been engaging in the scholarly critique of their religious tradition for decades and point out that an important legacy of women's activism in Judaism exists. Judith Baskin's 1991 book *Jewish Women in Historical Perspective* provides rich resources for understanding the roles and contributions of women throughout the religion's long history. Even just this broad characterization of traditions within Judaism shows that as in Christianity, so in Judaism one can find a full range of positions and perspectives on issues like women in leadership and restrictions on sexuality.

Questions about women's rights and roles within Islam is complicated by a difference of theology as well as by the political history of the religion's existence and a set of misperceptions that infect the West. While there are divisions within the religious tradition of Islam, most notably Sunni and Shi'a, the political and cultural distinctions between countries and regions are often more definitive for women in the religion. The early twenty-first century also brings with it the reality of Western occupation of Muslim countries that affects any discussion of Islam by those of us in the West. Specifically, Laura Bush's radio address in November 2001 linked the U.S. invasion of Afghanistan, a proportionate response to the country that harbored al Qaeda after the 9/11 terrorist attacks, to the liberation of women: "The fight against terrorism is also a fight for the rights and dignity of women."[26] This attempt to justify

25. Eisen, "Letter to the JTS Community," par. 1.; and Alpert, "Same Sex Marriage and the Law."

26. Bush, "Radio Address," para. 4.

military exercises by tying them to the liberation of women in Muslim cultures was not a new tactic; it had been used by the British colonial empire throughout the nineteenth and early twentieth century. Because of this history, Western discourse about the status of women in Islam is affected by cultural baggage and lack of historical awareness. More information about contemporary reality and the religion itself is required in order for Westerners to speak intelligently about the place of women in Islam.

One source for information about the Muslim world today is *The Gallup World Poll*, which includes data from more than 130 countries and areas, including face-to-face interviews with people in thirty-five nations that are predominantly Muslim. This sample represents "more than 90% of the world's 1.3 billion Muslims."[27] Among other things, the data show that "majorities of women in virtually every country we surveyed say that women deserve the same legal rights as men, to vote without influence from family members, to work at any job they are qualified for, and even to serve in the highest levels of government."[28] In addition, the majority of men in the Muslim world agree, though sometimes in slightly lower percentages (e.g., in Iran, 87 percent of men and 91 percent of women believe that women should be allowed to vote).[29] The polling also found no correlation between the degree of religiosity and disagreement with women's equality. In fact, contrary to popular assumption, the report points out that "in Lebanon, Morocco, and Iran, men who support women's rights are found to be more religious than those who do not

27. Esposito and Mogahed, *Who Speaks for Islam?* xi.
28. Ibid., 101–2.
29. Ibid., 121.

support women's rights."[30] Information like this goes a long way toward dispelling presumptions about Islam and about Muslim attitudes toward women.

One reason for these seemingly progressive attitudes is the sincere belief by many Muslims that Islam is fundamentally a religion based on justice and the equality of all humans before God. Scholars of the religion make this case. Amina Wadud as well as many other Islamic experts point out that the meaning of the term *islam* is "surrender," and the only one to whom Muslims fully surrender is Allah. To have to surrender to another human being would violate the order of creation. For that reason alone, Islam presents a theological picture in which men and women and all persons are on equal footing under Allah. This theology is often misconstrued and misunderstood by Westerners, leading to false assumptions about the source of oppression for women in Islamic countries.

At the same time, most traditions of Islam do not allow women to be imams, or public leaders in prayer services, though there has been activism on this front by women like Wadud. It also remains painfully true that women in Islamic countries suffer persecution and gender-based violence. In many of these cases, distinguishing the source of women's oppression as religious or political is difficult, in part because of the theocratic nature of Islam: the Taliban in Afghanistan wants to prevent girls from going to school, and one was assaulted with acid for trying to do so in 2008;[31] Wahhabi leaders in Saudi Arabia do not allow women to drive; after the 1979 Islamic revolution in Iran, women's lives were increasingly restricted and their public movements controled; mandates

30. Ibid., 123.
31. Khan, "10 Taliban Arrested."

for public dress in some Muslim countries disproportion-ately burden women; after decades of wars in Iraq, millions of widows are left to live in poverty amid destruction and desolation.[32] The intimate relationship of religion and politics makes it difficult to solely blame Islam for these realities, and it is clear that like Christianity, Islam has a mixed legacy when it comes to the treatment of women.

Beyond the Western world and Abrahamic religions, there are a vast array of religions cut from wholly different cultural and historical cloth. Buddhism and Hinduism share some territory and ideology, while religions such as Shinto and Jainism exist in relatively smaller numbers and more isolated contexts. Exploration of topics related to women in these religions does not fit easily into the categories like leadership, equality, and sexuality that have so far been dis-cussed. Hinduism, for example, has a wide array of gods and goddesses, who play different roles in the world and in the heavens. It does not have one founder or single set of beliefs that are easily evaluated, having emerged in India over the past several thousand years. The caste system of Hinduism mitigates against full human equality for many people, not just women, and the cultural record of India's treatment of women includes female infanticide as well as low female lit-eracy and marriage of young girls.

Nevertheless, India and Hinduism contain a range of opposing realities and beliefs about women, including that women serve at the highest levels of government as well as that women have some of the lowest standards of living in the world. A U.N. Report on the status of women in India showcases some of these seeming contradictory facts: the

32. I.R.I.N., "Iraq: Widow Numbers Rise," para. 4.

majority of women in India live their entire lives in a state of "nutritional stress," while India elected a female prime minister and was one of the first countries in the world to give women the right to vote.[33] India is a vast and varied country, and Hinduism has been a major factor in the culture. Again we are left with the question of how much the religion has affected the social and material conditions of women's lives.

Buddhism's emphasis on selflessness, acting with good intentions, and a nontheistic set of beliefs can suggest a religion with less embedded sexism than Western and monotheistic religions. It is also true that Buddhism contains prescriptions and rituals based on the presumed uncleanness of women, especially when they are menstruating. Such a view has been common to a variety of religions historically, when women's bodily functions were less scientifically understood and more culturally taboo. At the same time, Buddhists sometimes claim that theirs was the first major world religion to recognize the full spiritual equality of women and men, and women are now ordained as nuns at several levels within some forms of Buddhism.[34] Again, a mixed picture emerges with women's full equality existing alongside traditions and practices that suggest male superiority.

From this wide-ranging collection of examples and information from religions around the world, concluding whether Christianity is better or worse for women is nearly impossible. The treatment and views of women in any religion are inevitably tied to specific factors like time, place, family,

33. Menon-Sen and Kumar, "Women in India: How Free? How Equal?" 7-8.

34. Buddha Dharma Education Association, "Buddhism and Women."

resources, and politics. No religion has a fully negative or fully positive legacy when it comes to women's lives. One thing that is clear is that the status of women in all religions ranges from wholly oppressed or excluded to wholly affirmed and included. Insofar as religions around the world and throughout history have contributed to both the affirmation and denigration of women, they all deserve careful attention from feminists in the third wave.

Christianity is incredibly similar to other religions when it comes to women: A wide range of views and treatment of women has always been connected to an intricate set of historical and political factors that can both completely affirm as well as completely subordinate and mistreat women.

Suggested Reading

Judith Baskin, editor. *Jewish Women in Historical Perspective.* 1991.

John Esposito and Daria Mogahed. *Who Speaks for Islam?* 2007.

Rita Gross and Rosemary Radford Ruether. *Religious Feminism and the Future of the Planet.* 2001.

Amina Wadud. *Quran and Woman: Rereading the Sacred Text from a Woman's Perspective.* 1999.

TWO

Christian Questions of Feminism

Christians have many questions about feminism in part because feminism has directly challenged and even undermined some of its long-held beliefs and practices. Why would churches pay much attention to a secular ideology that seems to threaten traditions that have been around for thousands of years? Christianity has survived throughout the generations because it has been able to hold firm to its core commitments, and not be swayed by the ever-changing sea of culture around it. In addition, Christians believe that they have access to the revealed word of God in Scripture, which serves as the true test for any idea about God, the world, and what it means to be human. Whenever feminism seems to contradict the Bible, surely feminism is wrong.

The questions in this section capture some of this suspicious attitude that Christians have toward feminism, and the answers explain in more depth and detail what feminism is and what feminists care about in a way that shows its relevance for Christianity. Common stereotypes about feminists are addressed, and the complexity of Christianity is discussed so that Christians who believe that only one form of their religion exists might gain a broader perspective. In addition, implications of integrating feminism and Christianity are considered, whether it be a person's self-identifying as both Christian and feminist or the issue of women's ordination to church leadership.

The answers in this section take a critical look at the emergence of feminism and present the conviction that even with its flaws and limits, feminism is something that Christianity simply cannot afford to ignore or demonize. Christians have demonstrated the importance of faith seeking understanding from their humble beginning, and engagement with feminism is simply part of that ongoing quest.

2.1 WHY SHOULD CHRISTIANS CARE ABOUT FEMINISM?

Myths and stereotypes fuel the resistance that Christians have toward feminism. Stripping them away is a first step toward seeing why feminism matters, and why in fact it is good for Christianity. Feminists are not the man-hating, family-destroying feminazis that conservative ideologues like Rush Limbaugh believe them to be. Feminism is the radical idea that women are equally human, and Christians everywhere should care that throughout human history, and still today, people have not in fact believed or acted as if this were the case.

In twenty-first-century America, it is moderately easy to believe that women are fully human and entitled to the same rights and responsibilities as men: Women compose the majority of students in many American colleges and universities; a woman anchors the evening news on a major television network; a woman serves as speaker of the House of Representatives; the Episcopal church has a woman as presiding bishop; three of the most recent four U.S. secretaries of state have been women; women's purchasing power is regularly tapped by advertisers and corporations.

However, even in the twenty-first century, the following are still true: Women make up about 17 percent of the United States Congress. Women do not have to register for selective service at the age of eighteen as men do. Women are not allowed to serve in frontline combat positions even when qualified to do so. Every U.S. president has been male. All but three Supreme Court justices have been male. One in four women is raped or assaulted by an intimate partner at some point in her lifetime.[1] Studies still show that women earn approximately 77 cents for every dollar that men earn.[2] In the 2010 Vancouver Olympics, women are still prevented from competing in the ski jump despite the fact that that jump site's record holder is a woman.[3] Women cannot be ordained into leadership in the Roman Catholic Church, the Lutheran Church–Missouri Synod, the Christian Reformed Church, and many other sizable Christian denominations.

Women have indeed come a significant distance from cultures in which and eras when husbands were allowed to beat their wives with anything smaller in circumference than a thumb; when women were traded as commodities between their fathers and husbands; when women were not allowed to own, buy, or sell property in their own names; and when women's role in procreation was seen as entirely passive. Beliefs and practices that we would not legally or publicly allow today were upended in part because of feminism and

1. Tjaden and Thoennes, "Extent, Nature, and Consequences of Intimate Partner Violence," iii.

2. U.S. Census Bureau, "Household Income Rises," para. 9.

3. Berkes, "Gender Barrier," para. 1.

the women's movement. Despite that fact, even many women still resist the idea of feminism in part because of the negative stereotypes associated with it, and also because they personally don't feel oppressed. Recognizing the important and culturally beneficial work that feminism has done for both women and men takes little more than a cursory glance at history. Realizing that feminism is one reason why multitudes of women have had access and choices that they have had is important. Understanding how multitudes of women around the world and in our own neighborhoods still do not have all of the privileges afforded to men is also important. Feminism and the advocacy for women's equality remain culturally and politically relevant and necessary.

When feminism is understood as part of a movement to establish and preserve the equal humanity of women, and when the ways in which women are still not viewed or treated as fully human are comprehended, perhaps then Christians can see how it matters to them. Of course, objection to this basic claim surfaces quickly when Christians begin questioning and objecting to some feminist advocacy for specific things like access to contraception, which counters the official teaching of the Roman Catholic Church, and safe and legal abortion, which challenges the beliefs of many Christian individuals and denominations. In response to this, it is helpful to look an example of feminism and Christianity working together on an issue that often divides thee two spheres. The Evangelical Lutheran Church in America issued a social statement on abortion in 1993 that holds up fairly well to scrutiny from feminists as well as Christians over a decade and a half later. In this statement, the church insisted that Christians recognize the dignity and value of both the unborn and developing life as well as the woman "and her other relationships . . . Both the life of the woman and the life in her womb must be respected by law."[4] In doing so, the church remains committed to the value of all life, and ultimately trusts women and families with their decisions.

When so much of the public discourse about abortion excessively focuses on fetal rights, the ELCA statement takes steps not to forget the actual context of that fetal life: a woman. The denomination bases its position in part on the belief that her life is also a gift from God and must be protected, while recognizing the social conditions like poverty and violence against women that create the very question of abortion. Accounting for women's experience has only recently become a factor in Christian church's positions on issues like abortion due in large measure to the advocacy of feminism. The idea that women who need access to abortion are selfish baby killers is a crass, generalized falsehood, contrary to Christian theological claims that women are created in the image of God. It also ignores what Christianity recognizes as a fallen creation: Women who need access to abortion often need it because of fractured and violent relationships, lack of access to economic resources, inadequate health care, dangerous addictions, ignorance about the consequences of their actions, and unsuitable living conditions. Christianity takes seriously this brokenness of human life, feminism takes women's experiences of that brokenness seriously, and these situations reflect precisely that.

This example of one denomination's statement on abortion shows one way that Christianity is better equipped to respond to and engage with contemporary life when it learns

4. Evangelical Lutheran Church in America, "Abortion," para. 7.

with and from movements like feminism. In addition, feminism has shaped the character of Christianity to be more diverse and welcoming to more people in leadership; many mainline Protestant denominational seminaries now regularly enroll more women than men in their degree-granting programs. Women are serving churches around the country and around the world, and are in many cases moving up the ranks of local and national leadership structures. In 2006, the Episcopal Church USA elected its first female presiding bishop, Katharine Jefferts Schori.

Opening church leadership positions to women is only one part of the impact that feminism has had on Christianity. Rich academic theological work is being done by women in all sorts of Christian traditions, and many expressions of Christianity present a more welcoming and diverse theology because of it. Better knowledge of biblical texts, early Christian history, and the ways that cultural prejudices have crept into the religious tradition enables all Christians and their churches to be more faithful to the justice-oriented vision of God manifest in the life and teachings of Jesus. It also enables them to participate in creating more just and equitable human communities, and makes Christianity more accessible to those outside of it when the religion is able to be relevant to human experience in the contemporary world.

Some feminist scholarly work reads women back into the Christian tradition, and even pop culture has reflected this. The immense popularity of Dan Brown's 2003 novel *The Da Vinci Code* brought out hostility from those who cared more about preserving the ideology and history of male-dominance in Christianity. It also gave rise to curiosity from those who were intrigued by the very hypothesis of the powerful role of Mary Magdalene in the life and ministry of Jesus. In a discussion about the book I had with undergraduate students in class, I heard reactions that ranged from "It is just too dangerous to speculate about these things!" to "So what if Jesus was married? Good for him!" The fact that the book became a major pop-cultural phenomenon spawning all manner of anti–*Da Vinci Code* books like *The Da Vinci Hoax: Exposing the Errors In The Da Vinci Code* (2004), and *Rejecting "The Da Vinci Code": How A Blasphemous Novel Brutally Attacks Our Lord and the Catholic Church* (2005), suggests that ideas about powerful women in the history of Christianity simultaneously are exciting to some and remain threatening to many others.

Feminism has been a force for substantive and strategic changes in the modern history of Christianity, and those changes have been welcomed by some and resisted by others. Insofar as feminism is a movement for justice and equality, Christianity should recognize the ways that it has benefitted from feminist ideas and activism. Women have moved from being passively included in the life of the church to being active members and leaders throughout the religion. Christianity is more relevant and more inclusive in this millennium because of the critical and constructive attention from feminism.

Christians should care about feminism because it brings the religion back to the root ideals of egalitarian human life glimpsed in its early years, and because feminism has contributed to revitalizing the religion by advocating the leadership and scholarly contributions of women.

SUGGESTED READING

Estelle Freedman. *No Turning Back: The History of Feminism and the Future of Women*. 2003.

Lynn Japinga. *Feminism and Christianity: An Essential Guide*. 1999.

Joni Seager. *The Penguin Atlas of Women in the World*. 4th ed. 2008.

2.2 WHY DON'T FEMINISTS ACCEPT THAT THE BIBLE TEACHES THAT MEN AND WOMEN HAVE DIFFERENT ROLES IN CREATION, AND THAT WIVES SHOULD SUBMIT TO THEIR HUSBANDS?

Traditional Christian teachings like the idea that men and women have different roles spelled out in Genesis, and that wives should submit to their husbands as stated in Ephesians have supported patriarchal views that women are not equally human. This is clearly contrary to a basic feminist idea that women and men are equally human and is contrary to other Christian teachings about the dignity of every human being. These views have helped make the abuse of wives acceptable throughout history and have lent credibility to practices that reinforce women's second-class citizenship. Feminists do not accept these things as consequences of Christian teaching, and Christians should not accept them either. The two specific texts mentioned here are complicated in themselves, and a closer look reveals historical, theological, and sociological questions that both feminists and Christians should explore.

Specific questions about the history and authorship of Genesis 1–11 and Ephesians raise broader questions about the authority of biblical texts. To say that Scripture is authoritative for Christians is not necessarily to say that there is one clear and literal meaning of each text accepted by everyone. Every reader and hearer of a biblical text today is receiving something that is the product of a complicated process: An author was inspired to write the text in order to communicate something about God and the world. That author was also influenced and limited by the time and place in which he lived, and this context influenced how the stories were told. The stories survived in some form through oral transmission as well as copying and eventually translating from their original Hebrew or Greek to Latin, and eventually to German and English and Spanish and Chinese and many other languages.

Beyond the resulting complications in the text itself, interpretations emerge over time that make sense of a text in a new time and place, with new questions based in part on new insight into God, the world, and the human condition. This living tradition of making meaning out of ancient texts and stories is biblical interpretation. Christians today, therefore, are both the recipients of this tradition as well as participants in its continual unfolding. Attention to feminist insights when it comes to making meaning out of texts is part of the process of answering this question about Genesis and Ephesians in particular.

Genesis 1–11, the primordial history, is widely regarded by Christian and Jewish biblical scholars to function as a myth of origins similar to other creation narratives in the ancient world. There are many parallels between it and other ancient texts like the Epic of Gilgamesh, and scholars generally concur that the text is not an actual description of how humans and the earth came to exist. Scientific evidence and ongoing research further inform contemporary Christians and scholars looking at this primordial history. The narrative of the fall in chapter 3 of Genesis can be read as a story that reflected the world as its author knew it. His account of the human situation was descriptive (telling how things were for him) rather than prescriptive (telling how things ought to be for all time). This text, like all others in Scripture, reflects the author's situation and seeks to communicate a truth about God's relationship to the world, rather than a social ordering of male and female to be continued for all time.

Historical examination of Ephesians suggests that it was not written by the same author as were the indisputably authentic Pauline letters like Romans and Galatians. The likelihood of its later first-century composition, unique stylistic turns, as well as its view of a hierarchically ordered world and society are at odds with the contention of its being authored by Paul. Ephesians reflects the worldview of a later student of Paul's, and as such reflects a shifting social landscape where rigid hierarchies were being increasingly imposed. Considering the possibility that authors other than Paul, living in social worlds other than Paul's, wrote some letters attributed to him helps Christians to understand how specific texts in Ephesians, for example, apparently contradict others in Galatians.

Beyond questions about the historical origin and authorship of these texts, theological traditions of making meaning from them continue to have influence over what Christians think these passages say. Classic interpretations of the first three chapters of Genesis suggest that woman was and is a temptress who brought evil into the world, whose punishment is to submit to her husband. In the garden in Genesis

3:6, after the woman has a discussion about the tree with the serpent, "she took of its fruit and ate; and she also gave some to her husband who was with her, and he ate." Many questions about this narrative remain unanswered: Was she tricked? Did the serpent lie? Why didn't the man stop her? Did God lie? Answers to those questions challenge the meaning classically attached to Genesis 3.

Alternatives to the traditional "woman-caused-the-fall" meaning of the text do exist, and feminists are not even the first or only ones to offer different readings of biblical texts: Steven Kepnes describes Eve as the one "who boldly interprets the word of God and follows her senses," suggesting that the rabbinical tradition of midrash fills out Eve's character in a much more complex and active manner;[5] Irenaeus of Lyons in the second century read the story not as "the fall" but rather as "the rise" of humans, who are born naïve and then grow and progress into spiritual maturity and adulthood. It becomes easy to see how the theological meaning of this narrative has been under constant and shifting scrutiny by people of faith for millennia. Feminist questions about its meaning and implications continue to shed new light on the text.

The theological meaning of Ephesians, especially in the household codes section of 5:21—6:9, is equally as complex. Beginning with an injunction for all persons to be subject to one another, the passage specifically states: "Wives, be subject to your husbands as you are to the Lord. For the husband is the head of the wife just as Christ is the head of the church, the body of which he is the Savior. Just as the church is subject to Christ, so also wives ought to be, in everything, to

5. Kepnes, "Adam/Eve," para. 17.

their husbands" (Ephesians 5:22–24). The passage goes on to specify that husbands are to love their wives so that "she may become holy." The footnote in the *HarperCollins Study Bible* simply states regarding verse 24, "Nowhere do the undisputed Pauline Letters call for the subjection of wives."[6] Setting this passage apart from other Pauline texts is one way of making sense out of its potentially harmful suggestions, because it locates the teaching in a much different social context than our own, and even a different social context than the author of Galatians.

Some Christians emphasize that this passage is primarily about all Christians submitting to God, and that to read it as a justification for men's abuse of women is a tragic mistake. Sandra Clements is one of many evangelical Christian scholars who, even while adhering to the traditional claim that Paul authored Ephesians, spells out why submission as it is described in this text does not translate to license to dominate and abuse: "Submission, then, is volitional, and the sole purpose is to reflect Christ Jesus. It is without respect to age, gender, sex, nationality, and economic status. This submission I call Biblical Submission because it reflects the character of God: it is totally inclusive."[7] She goes on in her article to discuss the Greek terms used for submission and obedience, as well as the meaning of *submission* in the ancient military world, to contextualize the use of the term in this text. Many feminists would challenge the very credibility of "voluntary" submission in a patriarchal culture that rewards passive and submissive women. However, Clements' approach represents another way of interpreting the text in a way that does not

6. Attridge, ed. Ephesians 5:24n, 1989.
7. Clements, "Submission," para. 5.

sanction male domination of women while accepting its Pauline authorship. In this case also, the text is decidedly not a justification for abuse.

Feminists have been criticizing the social consequences of strictly defining and limiting women's and men's roles for generations. Carole R. Bohn makes this connection between history, social reality, and theology: "Throughout history, laws of various societies have attempted to limit the extent and means of man's control, but the underlying message, built into the words and structures of religious tradition, remains constant. By God's design, women and children are subject to men."[8] Feminists help Christians to see how this "theology of ownership" has functioned, and to ask questions that challenge its legitimacy: Should a wife submit to a husband who hits her in the face with a rolling pin? Is a wife required to forgive a husband who regularly visits prostitutes without her consent? Should children honor parents who lock them in a closet and deprive them of food for two weeks as punishment for spilling their cereal? Feminists point out that the problem is very simple: a teaching that requires one person to unqualifiedly submit to another person sanctions domination and subordination. This is not the promotion of the full humanity of women or of men. Both feminism and Christianity have been against the denigration of human beings and their dignity and should continue to be so.

Feminists are committed to the recognition of women's full equality with men, and wifely submission is not part of that picture. Equality does not have to mean sameness, however. For feminists, women's full equality means equal access

8. Bohn, "Dominion to Rule, 105.

to rights and privileges within the family, the workplace, and the legal system, in education and in politics. The power differential between men and women under patriarchy, as well as the value attached to the differences between men and women, is what many feminists have focused on and have worked to change. Biblical texts and theological traditions that support a patriarchal society remain problematic and require scrutiny from all Christians.

Feminists and Christians learn through closer historical, theological, and sociological examination that biblical texts and religious teachings against the full equality of men and women are limited by their contexts in their ability to communicate truth.

Suggested Reading

Joanne Carlson Brown and Carole R. Bohn, editors. *Christianity, Patriarchy, and Abuse: A Feminist Critique.* 1989.

Katharine Bushnell. *God's Word to Women.* 1921, reprinted in 2003. See also the related Web site with updated resources: http://www.godswordtowomen.org/main.htm/.

Robert M. Grant. *Irenaeus of Lyons.* 1996.

Linda S. Schearing, et al., editors. *Eve and Adam: Jewish, Christian, and Muslim Readings on Genesis and Gender.* 1999.

2.3 Isn't Feminism Just a Lot of Whining, Privileged, White Women?

A careful look at the history of feminism reveals that in earlier generations in particular it tended to be dominated by white, educated, and middle-class women who often failed to take the experiences of poor women and women of color fully into account. However, like Christianity, feminism is a tradition that has reformed over time and continues to adapt to the reality that surrounds it. Beginning in the late 1970s and increasingly throughout the 1980s, women of color began using the tools of feminism to challenge the movement to more fully include their reality. This included calling for a closer look at women's lives across the spectrum of race, class, sexuality, ability, age and many other aspects of experience. The third wave of feminism is now characterized by attention to the intersectional identity of all women and men that leads to multi-issue activism. Because of this, feminism has a different complexion than it did a generation or two ago and has a new set of insights relevant for Christianity.

In the first wave of feminism, women agitating for the vote paid little attention to the reality of life for women of color and working class women. Many suffragists were also abolitionists, yet their advocacy on behalf of slaves and former slaves did not translate directly into including women of color in their work. Tendencies to romanticize figures like Sojourner Truth are seen in the work of white women like Harriet Beecher Stowe and Frances Dana Gage. Gage authored a description of Truth's 1851 speech to the Women's Right's Convention in Akron, Ohio, in 1863, the same year that Stowe published an article describing an interaction she had with Truth. Both pieces depict Truth as "this almost Amazon form," who had "the magical influence that subduued [sic] the mobbish spirit of the day" [9] and who "wore a bright Madras handkerchief, arranged as a turban, after the manner

9. Gage, "Ain't I A Woman?" para. 5.

of her race."[10] These romanticized descriptions of Truth were likely constructed by the authors in order to appeal to the white readership of their publications. Nevertheless, criticism of nineteenth-century white feminist activism did exist, and one example can be discerned from remnants of Truth's Akron speech.

The original version of the speech reported by Marcus Robinson in 1851 is less poetic than Gage's famous "Ain't I a Woman?" legend, but contains similar sentiments. Robinson reports that Truth said, "I am a woman's rights. I have as much muscle as any man, and can do as much work as any man. I have plowed and reaped and husked and chopped and mowed, and can any man do more than that?"[11] Truth described a woman's life that was radically different from the lives of the upper-class white women leading the convention, making perhaps an even more compelling argument for the full equality of women and men. Segregation and class division produced the general lack of awareness that many early white feminist activists had about the lives of working-class women and women of color. Their fragmentary theological work and biblical criticism were similarly limited when it spoke of women's experience. Elizabeth Cady Stanton in particular has since been harshly criticized for the anti-Semitism laced throughout *The Woman's Bible*.

All this began to change during the second wave of feminism in the late 1970s and early 1980s. After Audre Lorde's public challenge to white feminists described in the introduction to this book, feminist theologians began taking criticisms like hers to heart and began incorporating race

10. Stowe, "Sojourner Truth," para. 3.
11. Robinson, "On Women's Rights," para. 2.

and class awareness into their work. Elizabeth Johnson in her 1992 book *She Who Is*, repeatedly sets forth this criteria for judging the adequacy of any theological idea or image: "For me the goal of feminist religious discourse pivots in its fullness around the flourishing of poor women of color in violent situations."[12] Consistent with the Christian gospels' and Hebrew Scriptures' portrayal of Jesus and God as regularly opting for the poor and siding with the marginalized, Johnson's feminist theology began to take seriously criticism by women of color. She used the experience of the most marginalized human beings as the ultimate test for any theological idea or religious practice.

Womanist theology emerged out of this nexus of religious scholars focusing on race and gender, and brought a necessary class sensibility with it. The term *womanist* is borrowed from Alice Walker's 1983 collection of prose called *In Search of Our Mother's Gardens*, in which she describes a womanist as, among many other things, "a black feminist or feminist of color."[13] Delores S. Williams and Jacquelyn Grant are theologians who critique feminism for its racist assumptions while critiquing black liberation theology and the black church for sexism and homophobia. In her 1995 book *Sisters in the Wilderness*, Williams examines the meaning of motherhood as it differs in the experiences of white women and black women. Looking at antebellum and postbellum motherhood experiences of black women, and correlating them with the Genesis story of Sarah's surrogate Hagar, Williams lends a creative interpretation both to a biblical text as well as to women's experiences. In short, like black women in the nine-

12. Johnson, *She Who Is*, 11.
13. Walker. *In Search of Our Mothers' Gardens*, xi.

teenth century, Hagar experienced forced surrogacy under slavery, as well as life-threatening conditions after the official end of slavery that made voluntary submission to a master a necessary means of sustaining her child. Beyond that, "Hagar, like many black women, goes into the wide world to make a living for herself and her child, with only God by her side."[14]

In pointing out the contemporary relevance of this history and this biblical text, Williams asks a series of questions about reproductive technology and the race/class bind for women today: "Can black women again be used by groups more powerful than they to produce children for the profit of more powerful groups? Will the law legitimate surrogacy to the point that black women's ovaries are targeted for use by groups more powerful than poor black women?"[15] The text provides an ancient framework for thinking about the divisions between women that continue to exist, about women who are free and enslaved in a host of subtle as well as not so subtle ways. Williams shows what difference it makes for making meaning out of biblical texts when theologians engage particular women's experiences.

A new generation of theologians is building on the womanist tradition, enlivened by Williams and others. They are also questioning the meaning and possibility of womanism in the twenty-first century, seen in a thought-provoking series of essays in the roundtable discussion prompted by Monica Coleman's 2006 essay "Must I Be a Womanist?"[16] Coleman and others describe a new generation, perhaps a third wave, of black, female religion scholars who weigh the options of

14. Williams, *Sisters in the* Wilderness, 33

15. Ibid., 82.

16. Coleman, et al., "Roundtable Discussion," 85–134.

embracing or criticizing the label *womanist*. They discuss a perceived hesitance of earlier womanists to fully discuss female homosexuality, womanism's assumed Christianity, and a perceived lack of political consciousness that has raised these questions about a new generation's identifying as womanist. Coleman ultimately suggests that "the term *womanist* may now be larger than the women who initially claimed it."[17] Here we find yet another tradition that has emerged and reformed over time.

Once the particularity of women's experiences was opened up in the way that Audre Lorde famously called for, feminist theologies began to be expressed with a multitude of voices. Ada María Isasi-Díaz uses the term *mujerista* to name a theology that places Hispanic women's experience at the heart and center of Christianity. Examining issues like ethics, identity, and the role of the Bible in a community with history of military conquest and language wars leads her to focus on women's moral agency as a key for life "*en la lucha*" (in the struggle). Native American women like Andrea Smith (Cherokee) have added another voice to feminist conversations about reproductive health and women's rights, while challenging Christianity for its complicity in the genocide of native people around the globe. Anita C. Hill has joined with others to publicly challenge Christianity's ongoing exclusion of gays and lesbians from full participation in the life of the church through her own "irregular" ordination in 2001, and her ongoing ministry at St. Paul Reformation Lutheran Church in Minnesota. Hill is part of a much larger movement for the inclusion of gays and lesbians in all aspects of life in

17. Ibid., 93.

society and in Christian churches that transcends denomination and region.

Because feminism has emerged in the third wave as a multi-issue and multi-cultural movement dedicated to giving voice and access to women across the spectrum of human experience, Christianity benefits from connecting to it. Religion is one of the many aspects of human identity for feminism to engage in the twenty-first century. In addition, Christianity continues to grow in nonwhite and nonwealthy parts of the world, while it is stagnant or losing population in the white, developed world. Other religions of the world are powerful forces internationally, affecting the lives of women and men within their reach. Both feminism and Christianity are now paying long-overdue attention to the global human community, taking seriously their privileged positions by advocating for improving life in all contexts. Both traditions benefit and learn from each other by working together toward integrating visions of justice for all.

Feminism in the third wave is a global justice movement acting on behalf of women's full equality at the intersection of race, class, gender, and other aspects of identity, making it even more relevant for a global Christianity in the twenty-first century.

SUGGESTED READING

Monica A. Coleman, et al. "Roundtable Discussion: Must I Be a Womanist?" 2006.

Anita C. Hill and Leo Treadway. "Rituals of Healing: Ministry with and on behalf of Gay and Lesbian People." 1998.

Ada María Isasi-Díaz. *En la Lucha = In the Struggle: Elaborating a Mujerista Theology; A Hispanic Women's Liberation Theology.* 1993.

Audre Lorde. *Sister Outsider: Essays and Speeches.* 1996.

Delores S. Williams. *Sisters in the Wilderness: The Challenge of Womanist God-Talk.* 1993.

2.4 Do Feminists Just Want to Turn Patriarchy into a Matriarchy?

The problem identified in patriarchy is not necessarily men: Unqualified privileging of men over women is part of a system of dominating power and control, which carefully prescribes masculinity and femininity in a way that limits the humanity of all persons. With its focus on women's experience, feminism does not need to turn a patriarchy upside down and make it a matriarchy. In addition, feminism does not advocate the hating of men when it criticizes male dominance. Feminism brings with it a new way of conceiving of power relations between women and men, between people of different races and ethnicities, and between humans and the earth. All this has in fact been threatening to those who benefit the most from patriarchy: men. The common charge that feminists hate men and simply want women to run the world is usually meant to mock a movement that has produced complicated and systematic analysis of social problems.

Second-wave feminist theologian Mary Daly responded to attempts to dismiss feminism by naming several tactics used by patriarchy: Critics of feminism trivialize, particularize, spiritualize, or universalize the problem.[18] To trivialize the

18. Daly, *Beyond God the Father*, 4-6.

problem is to say that women are selfish and silly to look at such trivial issues as sexism in advertising when there are so many more important issues like global warming and children dying in poverty. To particularize the problem is to say that the problem of women's oppression is really just a problem for particular groups like Catholics or Baptists, when non-religious or only faintly religious people are much more tolerant. To spiritualize the problem is to say that in God's eyes everyone is equal in spirit, so a little suffering in this earthly life will not matter in the long run. Finally, to universalize the problem is to say that women aren't the only ones suffering; everyone universally suffers, and women are no different.

As Daly noted nearly forty years ago, these ways of "refusing to see the problem" are "overwhelming and insidious."[19] This is in part because each of the four points made here is not untrue, which makes carefully responding to them important. If we understand patriarchy as a system of dominating power and control that benefits men, then responding to each of these four criticisms entails a broader and more systemic analysis than just pitting men against women.

Next to the real problem of children orphaned by the AIDS pandemic in Africa, challenging sexism in advertising, for example, is trivial. A systemic analysis reveals, though, that constant visual clues, through advertising, that women are merely sexual objects for male consumption is one of the things that supports more egregious actions like limiting women's independence and controlling their rights. In some places, controlling women takes the form of prohibiting access to reproductive-health resources like condoms in high

19. Daly, *Beyond God the Father*, 6.

school, birth-control pills at college health centers, and emergency contraception at the local pharmacy. In fact, any sexual activity by women that takes place outside heterosexual marriage is then demonized, while a "boys-will-be-boys" attitude is granted to men, who have no similar restrictions and can do things like frequent prostitutes. When these emerging values about unfettered male and controlled female sexuality are lived out around the world, the results include millions dying from AIDS because of a lack of resources to prevent infection, limited education about the options that do exist, no access to health care, and little empowerment for women to control their own sexual activity. It is not trivial to focus on small things that contribute to a system that perpetuates big things.

It is also true that particular populations of women are more oppressed than others. Women in the developed Western world are by many accounts healthier and wealthier than previous generations, while women in developing nations continue to die in childbirth for reasons such as unsanitary birthing conditions. A systemic analysis quickly shows that lesser problems like whether or not the pharmacist at the well-stocked Walgreens less than a mile from my comfortable two-story house will provide emergency contraception without a hassle are supported by the same value system and practices that make the following fact true: "More than 80 per cent of maternal deaths worldwide are due to five direct causes: hemorrhage, sepsis, unsafe abortion, obstructed labour and hypertensive disease of pregnancy."[20] A large majority of these deaths are wholly preventable through safe and

20. The United Nations Population Fund, "Facts About Safe Motherhood," para. 4.

sanitary birthing conditions and access to basic natal and prenatal care. Next to the woman who suffers from obstetric fistula (a rupture in the vaginal wall usually caused by unsafe birthing and lack of medical care), my lack of access to emergency contraception does appear trivial, but both of us are oppressed under the same system that privileges men's health while ignoring or controlling women's health.

Evangelical Christians and even many feminist Christians quickly point to the same Galatians text discussed elsewhere in this book in order establish the equality of men and women: "there is no longer male and female; for all of you are one in Christ Jesus" (Galatians 3:28). Spiritual equality is a fine and helpful theological idea worth affirming and even celebrating. It does not make human inequality and a planetary crisis of resources untrue or negligible. Latin American liberation theologians like Gustavo Gutiérrez carefully described how Christianity failed the masses by excessively focusing on an eternal spiritual life with God. To ignore the quality of human life on earth right now dishonors the value of that life. What about people who do not believe that there will be another life? Even for those who do, does eternal happiness and bliss make it acceptable that Elisabeth Fritzl was locked in a dungeon for twenty-four years and raped and beaten by her father, Josef, who impregnated her seven times and burned the body of one infant who had died?[21] The answer must be a resounding no. Spiritual equality does not justify actual inequality.

Universalizing the problem of oppression, a final tactic of those who "refuse to see," attempts to dismiss the feminist

---

21. Naughton, "Elisabeth Fritzl Tells of Father's Cruelty," para. 2, 6.

focus on women's oppression by insisting that men suffer and are oppressed too. Men do suffer under patriarchy insofar as it presents a limiting notion of what it means to be a man and applies unattainable standards of achievement and strength to their lives. Race, class, education, and other sources of privilege and inequality affect men as well as women. One contemporary version of this universalizing impulse is recent focus on what some have labeled "the boy crisis." Authors and journalists at the turn of this century began touting the fact that boys and young men were falling behind girls and young women in academic performance, enrollment in colleges and universities, and measures of self-esteem. In a May 2000 article in *The Atlantic Monthly*, conservative writer Christina Hoff Sommers lifted up the images of Eric Harris and Dylan Klebold, the troubled trench-coated Columbine shooters, as the epitome of what was wrong for boys in American culture.[22] From lower test scores to higher drop-out rates and lower enrollment in colleges, boys now fare worse than girls in the U.S. educational system, she argued. Feminism's excessive focus on supporting women and girls, it seems, had ignored boys and had just gone too far for many who read and responded to Sommers' article.

Just as many authors and commentators picked up on this idea and ran with it, critics began to emerge. They pointed out other significant statistics that undercut the largely anti-feminist crowd promoting the idea that boys were now suffering more than girls because of feminism. The most compelling point remains that despite all this educational underperformance, men still significantly outperform women

22. Sommers, "The War against Boys."

in wage earning, business ownership, and political electability. A *Washington Post* article on April 9, 2006, as well as an American Association of University Women report in May 2008 indicate not only that the "crisis" is not the reality many authors have suggested, but that family income, race, and class are much more significant crisis indicators for both boys and girls in terms of education and development.[23] Boys and men do suffer under patriarchy insofar as their humanity is predefined and they are pressured to be conquerors, strong and silent, manly, and stoic. But reports of this crisis seem to have been greatly exaggerated.

Updated responses to these four classic attempts to undercut feminist criticism of patriarchal institutions like religion, education, and the family show how necessary systemic analysis is to understandings privilege and inequality. Christianity has participated in the system, and benefits from understanding how feminism offers a mode of understanding that serves the full and equal humanity of both women and men. Rather than trivialize, particularize, spiritualize, or universalize "the problem" under patriarchy, feminism embarks on focused and systematic response to complicated issues at the intersections of gender, race, sexuality, and class. In this way, it is still not about hating men.

Feminism's focus on women names the problem of sexism and reality of inequality in society and in the church, challenging a system that values and grants power to some people over others on the basis of unearned privileges.

---

23. American Association of University Women, *Where the Girls Are*; and Rivers and Barnett, "The Myth of the Boy Crisis."

SUGGESTED READING

American Association of University Women. *Where the Girls Are: The Facts about Gender Equity in Education.* 2008.

Ian Sample. "Sex Objects: Pictures Shift Men's View of Women." 2009.

The United Nations Population Fund. Web site. Online: http://www.unfpa.org/public/. 2009.

2.5 HOW CAN A PERSON BE BOTH CHRISTIAN AND FEMINIST?

There is nothing inherently contradictory about these two identities, especially when one considers carefully how the terms *Christian* and *feminist* are understood. Definitions from certain persons and groups within each movement can and do exclude members of the other from it: Some Christians argue that feminism is part of what is wrong with an increasingly secular world; Some feminists argue that Christianity is nothing more than the handmaiden of patriarchy. If those were the only positions, it would in fact be impossible to be both Christian and feminist. Many Christians and feminists think of their beliefs and commitments in such a way that there can be a natural connection between the two parts of their identity. Specific topics like individual human dignity and equality, a just human community, and a peaceable relationship between humans and the earth provide much common ground between Christianity and feminism.

While they use different language for describing the inherent worth of every person, and may differ in their understanding of the implications of the idea, Christians and feminists share a core belief here. Christianity borrows language from Genesis to say that all humans are created in the image of God: "So God created humankind in his image, in the image of God he created them; male and female he created them" (Genesis 1:27). The theological claim is that there is something of God in every individual person. Because of this, each one is to be valued for herself or himself. Feminism often uses rights language to represent the same idea: "Because feminism is politics of equality, it anticipates a future that guarantees human dignity and equality for all people, women and men."[24] The political importance of this claim is that if each person is treated as equally human, then each one is given the same access and privileges regardless of gender, race, or class.

A notable point of divergence on the implications of the idea of individual human dignity and equality should be noted here. For some Christians, the idea that each human being is valued and created in the image of God means that even unborn fetuses have the same rights and privileges as adult persons. They use this idea to trump the rights and moral agency of women who are pregnant, prohibiting abortion, for example, often in any case. Feminists for the most part, as well many Christians, disagree with this conclusion and opt to preserve the legality and safety of abortion as well as the moral agency of women to determine the best course of action for their own families.

For some feminists, the idea that each human being is to be treated with individual dignity leads to making the case for women's full participation in the leadership of their religion.

24. Shaw and Lee, *Women's Voices, Feminist Visions*, 9.

If there is no inherent difference in the worth and dignity of men and women, then women ought to have access to the same positions as men, including those of priest and bishop. Christians throughout history disagreed with this conclusion, and many still limit the office of pastor, priest, or bishop to male human beings. Some women also agree with this exclusion, either because they accept the patriarchal premise that women are not suited for leadership, or because they hold the divergent feminist premise that seeking leadership in patriarchal religions misses the point of women's liberation. These two examples show the sincere difference in conclusions reached by Christians and feminists ostensibly adhering to the same value: preserving the individual human dignity and equality of every person.

Forming and sustaining a just human community is another broad commitment shared by Christians and feminists, where a person identifying with both can find resonance. Feminists have a passionate focus on justice particularly in the area of gender equality and also in the areas of race, class, and sexuality. The just human community for feminists is one where each person participates fully, has his or her identity affirmed and celebrated, and is not prevented from attaining a fully flourishing life on the basis of any structural inequalities. Christians have long described the ideal human community as one where fellow participants love one another and are freed to serve their neighbor and praise God. Biblical texts that express such an idea abound, and Christian reformer Martin Luther lifted up this notion when he described "a truly Christian life. Here faith is truly active through love [Galatians 5:6], that is, it finds expression in works of the freest service, cheerfully and lovingly done, with which a man willingly serves another without hope of reward."[25] Such ideal pictures of the human community are common throughout Christianity.

On the idea of a just human community there are also points of conflict between Christians and feminists. While many feminists affirm the possibility of and necessary legality of same-sex relationships, Christianity has a complicated history of condemning the possibility. Where feminism eventually recognized its racist tendencies when they were pointed out, Christianity has moved more slowly toward racial justice and integration. Where Christianity holds that the just human community is possible because of a loving God who is the source of life for all beings, feminists argue that justice is primarily the work of human beings on behalf of human beings. Some of these ideas are contradictory, while some of these ideas are merely on different tracks.

Feminists and Christians in the twenty-first century also share an emerging commitment to a just and sustainable relationship between humans and the earth. In this century, any movement or religion that does not embrace and act on this imperative does so at its own peril. No longer can anyone afford to pretend that human actions do not imperil the planet, and that humans do not have a responsibility to preserve the environment. That does not mean that such damaging beliefs and ideas no longer exist. A small minority of Christians adhere to the historically dominant position of the religion: that the earth is here for humans to subdue and have dominion over, based on their reading of the text that begins with Genesis 1:28, which exhorts humans to "be fruitful and

25. Luther, "The Freedom of a Christian" 365.

multiply, and fill the earth and subdue it; and have dominion over the fish of the sea and over the birds of the air and over every living thing that moves upon the earth." Many more Christians, however, have moved in the necessary direction of reemphasizing the human role of stewardship. Rather than seeing this as a controlling mastery of the earth, Christian theologians have suggested seeing stewardship as a trustee-ship, in which humans are entrusted to care for the resources of the created world.

Feminists have been working toward incorporating an ecojustice element into their work since Rachel Carson's 1962 book *Silent Spring* plainly spelled out the consequences for human health of the misuse and overuse of pesticides. As part of a vision for present and future feminist activism, authors Susan Shaw and Janet Lee specify that "feminist integrity requires advocating a sustainable physical environment. There is only one world and we share it; there is an interdependence of all species."[26] While not a major focus in second-wave feminism and not at all a part of first-wave feminism, global and national environmental policies and practices have come under much scrutiny in more recent feminist work both theological and not. In her 1992 book *Gaia & God*, theologian Rosemary Radford Ruether shows how control of the earth and control of women are based on the same patriarchal assumptions. Through her writing and the work of her research founda-tion, leading ecofeminist Vandana Shiva criticizes patriarchy for supporting earth-destroying practices and advocates the empowerment of women. Wangari Maathai won the Nobel Peace Prize in 2004 for her work founding the Green Belt

26. Shaw and Lee, *Women's Voices, Feminist Visions*, 716.

Movement in Kenya, expanding environmental activism primarily through networks of women. Though they sometimes use different language and have a different emphasis from Christians who write and speak on the subject, feminists share with most Christians a commitment to sustaining the earth that all of us are damaging.

With these three broad thematic connections between Christianity and feminism, it is clear how one can be both a Christian and a feminist. Celebrating individual human dignity and equality, creating a just human community, and preserving the natural resources of this planet are obvious places to ground a Christian and feminist identity. Conversations between the two communities about their divergent interpretations of some of these commitments can lead to conflict, or it can lead to a deeper understanding of some shared common ground.

A person can be both Christian and feminist because the two identities share some core commitments to human dignity and equality, justice among people, and sustainable relationships with the earth.

Suggested Reading

Anne M. Clifford. *Introducing Feminist Theology.* 2001.

Mary Henold. *Catholic and Feminist: The Surprising History of the American Catholic Feminist Movement.* 2008.

Allyson Jule and Bettina Tate Pederson, editors. *Being Feminist, Being Christian: Essays from Academia.* 2008.

Rosemary Radford Ruether. *Gaia & God: An Ecofeminist Theology of Earth Healing.* 1992.

2.6 ARE ALL FEMINISTS REALLY LESBIANS? DOESN'T FEMINISM AT LEAST PROMOTE THE SIN OF HOMO- SEXUALITY?

Stereotyping feminists as lesbians is a tactic that has been used by opponents of the women's movement for genera- tions. That assumption, along with the one that Christianity universally and perennially teaches that homosexuality is a sin, requires careful study of derogative stereotypes, Christian history, and biblical texts to dispel rumors and distinguish fact from fiction.

The basic belief behind the suspicion that feminists are lesbians is that being a lesbian is a bad thing. A term has emerged for this fear-based attempt to dissuade women from identifying as feminist: *lesbian baiting*. Lesbian baiting works in a heterosexist and patriarchal culture where women are supposed to want to be appealing to men. In such a culture, the "accusation" of being a lesbian is the equivalent of social shunning. A woman so labeled does not fit into the accept- able role for women under patriarchy. It is true that there are feminists who are lesbians, though certainly not all lesbians would identify as feminists, further complicating the sup- posed equation of feminism and lesbianism.

Audre Lorde pointed out that "heterosexism is some- times a result of identifying with the white patriarchy, [which rejects] that interdependence between women-identified women which allows the self to be, rather than to be used in the service of men."[27] The danger of falling into the trap of identifying with the white patriarchy as Lorde describes it is that women are then dissuaded from forming bonds with

27. Lorde, "Age, Race, Class, and Sex," 121.

one another. Among other things, these bonds made the women's movement and feminism possible. This is why they are feared, and this is why they are needed. Lesbian baiting is the attempt to thwart these connections. The assumption that all feminists are lesbians simultaneously caricatures lesbians and threatens feminist advocacy on behalf of all women.

Feminism does in fact affirm human sexuality outside just the patriarchal and heteronormative model. Human sexuality takes many forms, and feminists recognize that it is expressed between consenting adults in a variety of healthy and acceptable ways. This idea is increasingly supported by evidence from the psychological and biological sciences. Heterosexism, privileging of the heterosexual over the homosexual, is a by-product of sexism, which itself is a product of patriarchy: Under patriarchy men are the privileged sex, and it is therefore less desirable to be a woman. In the ancient world, a sexual relationship between two men was taboo for some because it put one of the men in the role of a woman: he had to be the passive one and the receiver of male sex. This idea continues to exist today in less body-focused ways, for instance, it is a common insult for men to feminize each other. So male homophobia specifically emerges out of a patriarchal mindset and is expressed through such things as lesbian baiting.

General homophobia encompasses a fear of both male and female homosexuality and often uses Christianity and biblical teachings for religious justification. This is because it is assumed that Christianity uniformly teaches and has always taught that homosexuality is a sin. The religion has a more complicated legacy than many understand when it comes to homosexuality. John Boswell has written a definitive history of social tolerance in Christianity, focusing primarily on homosexuality as one example of a practice about which various sources of intolerance exist. He does so because "hostility to gay people provides singularly revealing examples of the confusion of religious beliefs with popular prejudice."[28] He shows through detailed historical cases how the religion was not in fact the primary or only cause of the intolerance of gay people; rather Christianity was used when convenient to justify prejudices. Refusing to accept the simple explanation that Christianity merely applies the Bible and God's word to human behavior, Boswell points out, "Biblical strictures have been employed with great selectivity by all Christian states."[29] He points out that social taboos and laws against hypocrisy, for example, did not emerge even though they were condemned even more stringently than homosexual acts in many of the exact same texts. One accomplishment of Boswell's study is to show complex factors affecting prejudice and intolerance throughout the premodern Christian world and therefore in our world today.

He also shows that Christianity and its early states in fact did not explicitly prohibit homosexuality, though it was occasionally stigmatized by some writers. In third-century Roman imperial law, for example, the standard for determining criminal sexual behavior was based on one's status as a citizen rather than the gender of one's partner. Roman culture also makes no consistent condemnation of homosexuality: "Neither Roman religion nor Roman law recognized homosexual eroticism as distinct from—much less inferior

28. Boswell, *Christianity, Social Tolerance, and Homosexuality*, 5-6.
29. Ibid., 7.

to—heterosexual eroticism."[30] More overt intolerance of homosexuality began to take hold with the rise of Christianity in the fourth century, but other factors like "autocratic oppression and increasingly rural ethics" were important contributors to the shift of views about acceptable sexual behaviors.[31] Boswell considers in great detail examples from literature, works of art, and case law over fourteen hundred years to challenge the assumption that Christianity has perennially condemned homosexuality and has done so only because of God's word. He says, "Neither Christian society nor Christian theology as a whole evinced or supported any particular hostility to homosexuality, but both [society and theology] reflected and in the end retained positions adopted by some governments and theologians which could be used to derogate homosexual acts."[32] Perhaps most important, Boswell forces Christians to recognize that other sources of prejudice affect cultural standards and personal views, and that their religious tradition is not historically homogenous.

Many Christians use biblical texts to "prove" conclusively that homosexuality is a sin and always has been. Daniel Helminiak has written a very accessible book called *What the Bible Really Says about Homosexuality*. In it he carefully shows the problem with using biblical texts in arguments against homosexuality by debunking traditional interpretations of passages like Genesis 19. This story of the destruction of Sodom and Gomorrah was classically read as a condemnation of homosexuality, even though homosexuality as we now understand it was a concept not even a part of the ancient

30. Ibid., 73.

31. Ibid., 120–24.

32. Ibid., 333.

worldview that informed the author of this and other texts. Helminiak uses evidence about the context of the ancient world and clues from other biblical references to the story to conclude that the sin of Sodom is not gay sex: "So what was the sin of Sodom? Abuse and offense against strangers. Insult to the traveler. Inhospitality to the needy."[33] This interpretation of the Sodom-and-Gomorrah story is now increasingly understood to be the more accurate reading, based on what we know about ancient cultures as well as corroborating claims about the sin of Sodom elsewhere in the Bible, including Jesus' own mention of it in Matthew 10.

Helminiak applies these tools of biblical study to every text that possibly mentions same-sex behavior. Using an understanding of ancient culture as well as a careful word study in Hebrew and Greek, he shows that the abomination referred to in Leviticus 18:22 is not male-male sex; it is uncleanness according to the ancient purity laws and their understanding of male and female roles. He also focuses on New Testament texts like the first chapter of Romans as well as 1 Corinthians and 1 Timothy. In all, he shows how a clearer understanding of history, careful study of the meaning of words in their ancient contexts, and a better understanding of the author's intent reveal each text to be about moral and social issues beyond homosexuality.

The complexities of Christianity's understanding of sexuality are here only introduced, and the tradition itself has a long way to go before it as a whole meshes easily with feminist affirmations of human sexuality in its many and varied forms. Uncovering the complicated history of the tradition (seeing that many factors contribute to social intolerance in

33. Helminiak, *What the Bible Really Says about Homosexuality*, 46.

any culture) and examining biblical texts in detail is a part of the ongoing, ever-reforming Christian tradition.

Several examples of the varying states of change within Christianity reveal a complicated present-day situation: The United Church of Christ fully affirms homosexuality as a natural part of human identity created by God, ordaining openly gay and lesbian individuals as well as affirming their marriages. Several mainline Protestant denominations like the Lutherans (ELCA), Presbyterians (PCUSA), and United Methodists have ongoing denominational studies, discussions, and closely contested national votes on issues like gay marriage and ordination. The Roman Catholic Church welcomes homosexual individuals into their churches while teaching that it is a sinful behavior that an individual should work to avoid. Several "ex-gay ministry" organizations like Exodus International exist in order to promote their idea that homosexuality is a sin and that individuals can be freed from it through faith in Jesus Christ. And at an extreme end of what some understand to be Christian churches, the Westboro Baptist Church under the leadership of Fred Phelps in Colorado has a motto proclaiming that "God Hates Fags." They organize protests at military and other high-profile funerals, and disruptions of gay-pride parades; they speak out on any event when they can gain attention for their claim that toleration of gay people leads to every evil that befalls the United States. As witnessed by this disparate list of Christian-church positions, the religion is still working out its options on the issue of human sexuality.

Feminism does affirm human sexuality in its varied forms, and Christianity has a complicated tradition of dealing with all issues related to human sexuality. This is an area where perhaps some of the greatest differences arise between the two spheres, opening up significant conflict as well as opportunity for conversation and transformation.

Debunking assumptions both about feminism as well Christianity when it comes to homosexuality leads to a realistic challenge to the religious tradition which some denominations are meeting and others are battling.

Suggested Reading

Estelle B. Freedman. *Feminism, Sexuality, and Politics.* 2006.

Daniel Helminiak. *What the Bible Really Says about Homosexuality.* Millennium ed., 2000.

Jeffrey Siker, editor. *Homosexuality in the Church.* 1994.

2.7 Does feminism include goddess worship? If so, isn't it anti-Christian?

Feminists have studied goddesses. Some feminists worship the Goddess. Some feminist theologians suggest new ways of naming God/ess that undercut patriarchal presumptions about the divine. Some feminists reject any notion of a divine being, male or female. While absolutely no consensus exists among feminists as to the name, meaning or existence of a divine being, feminists agree that Christianity's ideas about God must be examined. Women respond to the limits of and problems with a religion led by male human beings and subject to a male god by studying the history of the idea, transforming language about God, and incorporating new views into the worship life of Christian churches.

In ancient history, the emergence of patriarchy and monotheism depended on the literal and figurative suppression of various goddess-oriented religions and cultures. Riane Eisler, in her 1987 book *The Chalice and the Blade*, traces the transformation of cultures from those that valued the female and worshiped the goddess to those that taught strict obedience to a male god. She discusses Mesopotamian, Sumerian, and Babylonian cultures with their myths and legends about the Goddess as the source of all life, practices of female ownership and leadership, and partnership models for organizing society that predate Judaism and Christianity. She goes on to show how the rise of monotheism in particular brought with it practices and beliefs designed specifically to undercut these cultures, some of which were matrilineal and many of which were intentionally female affirming: "the vilification of the serpent and the association of women with evil were a means of discrediting the Goddess."[34] Eisler discusses the rise of biblical religion and how it systematically erased the Goddess, despite ongoing worship of her in various groups. She concludes that "interlaced with what is humane and uplifting, much of what we find in the Judeo-Christian Bible is a network of myths and laws designed to impose, maintain, and perpetuate a dominator system of social and economic organization."[35] What Eisler names "a dominator system" is patriarchy when men are the ones who benefit from the system, and who have nearly sole responsibility for designing and leading it.

This history reveals that Christianity is a religion of the male victors. For some women, this alone is a reason

34. Eisler, *The Chalice and the Blade*, 89.
35. Ibid., 94.

to abandon its male god and male-led structures. Other women respond by searching the tradition for options in naming and imaging God. Rosemary Radford Ruether's 1983 book *Sexism and God-Talk* presents a fully researched set of options and implications for "God-talk," showing how Christianity can incorporate ideas about God from what she calls five areas of "usable tradition." This includes Hebrew and Christian Scripture, marginalized Christian groups, dominant Christian theological traditions, and non-Christian and post-Christian sources. Applying a feminist lens to each of these areas, Ruether draws out their resources while critiquing their sexist tendencies.[36]

In her book *She Who Is*, Elizabeth Johnson focuses specifically on the issue of language for God, opting for female images and names for God for substantive and strategic reasons. In claiming the name "SHE WHO IS" for speaking of God, Johnson makes the case that it is linguistically possible, theologically legitimate, and existentially necessary. In addition, she notes that the symbol of "SHE WHO IS" stands as a political challenge to "every structure and attitude that assigns superiority to ruling men on the basis of their supposed greater godlikeness."[37] Johnson repeatedly points out that societies ascribe to their deity the traits and characteristics that they value most highly. The continued dominance of male images and language for God simply serves to reinforce patriarchy and is based on limited use of metaphors from Scripture, tradition, and human experience.

In part because of this problem, feminists like Nelle Morton and Carol Christ have opted instead to fully tap

36. Ruether, *Sexism and God-talk*, 21-46.
37. Johnson, *She Who Is*, 243.

into the Goddess in response to the patriarchal monotheism of Christianity. Morton describes her own unexpected and liberating experiences of the Goddess in the context of a women's conference on theology and also during a terrifying airplane flight. For her, "the Goddess ushered in a reality that respects the sacredness of my existence, that gives me self-esteem so I can perceive the universe and its people through my woman-self and not depend on the perception conditioned by patriarchal culture and patriarchal religion."[38] In addition to her thealogical discussions in *Rebirth of the Goddess* (1998), Christ constructs a feminist philosophy of religion based on a notion of divine power that is intimately connected to the world, changing with it and luring it toward truth, beauty, and goodness. She incorporates process philosophy with feminism to describe the divine in female form in her 2003 book, *She Who Changes*.

Two practical examples show how Christian churches are trying to realize these proposals either for inclusive language or for embracing the Goddess. The Presbyterian Church USA articulated its commitment to inclusive language in 1985 because, it said, "the diversity of culture, gender, class, and race, which is present in the church and in the world, often is not reflected in the language of the church." This statement spells out definitions of and guidelines for the use of inclusive language about human beings as well as about God because of "the church's emerging conviction both that the diversity of the people of God is to be acknowledged and embraced in such a way that all may feel included."[39] This strategy characterizes the responses of many mainline Christian denomina-

38. Morton, "The Goddess as Metaphoric Image," 195.
39. Presbyterian Church, "Response to Inclusive Language," para. 6.

tions to the feminist critique of exclusively male language and images of God.

The second option is more unique. Ebenezer/herchurch Lutheran, an ELCA congregation in San Francisco, embodies a new Christian identity. It remains connected to the tradition while proclaiming itself to be "a reconciling in Christ congregation; a house of prayer for all people; a home for women's spirituality." An additional statement from the church's Web site incorporates both the Christian tradition of which it is a part as well as creative feminist theological ideas: "Our Christian/Lutheran feminist prayers and liturgy reach back into the storehouse of tradition to bring forth names as Mother, Shaddai, Sophia, Womb, Midwife, Shekinah, She Who Is. They do so out of renewed insights into the nature of the Gospel empowered by the risen Christ-Sophia."[40]

Churches like this are the exception rather than the rule for this or for any other denomination. Ebenezer/herchurch provides an interesting example of a community trying to intentionally bridge its Christian and feminist identities specifically in worship practices that name and celebrate the Goddess.

In these ways, feminism is not about goddess worship; nor is it necessarily anti-Christian. It is more precise and more historically correct to say that Christianity became anti-Goddess as it developed in opposition to the idea of a female deity. The examples here show that feminists, theologians and philosophers among them, are reintroducing the idea of the Goddess into religious practice, even into Christian religious practice. This is not an option that all or even many Christians

40. Ebenezer/herchurch Lutheran, San Francisco, ELCA. Web page.

(including feminist Christians) would embrace, but it is one of the more intentional and challenging attempts to redefine religion as we know it. What these examples have in common is a critical assessment of the limitations of exclusively male language for a God who, Christians claim, is beyond human categories like gender.

Feminism challenges Christianity to understand its history of suppressing concepts of a female deity as well as to open itself up to a rich storehouse of images and names for God that more fully represents human experience.

SUGGESTED READING

Carol P. Christ. *Rebirth of the Goddess: Finding Meaning in Feminist Spirituality*. 1998.

Riane Eisler. *The Chalice and the Blade: Our History, Our Future*. 1987.

Elizabeth Johnson. *She Who Is: The Mystery of God in Feminist Theological Discourse*. 1992.

2.8 WHY DO WOMEN THINK THEY CAN BE PASTORS?

While less controversial than some other topics in Christianity today, the ordination of women remains a contested issue for many denominations. A brief review of the history of major denominations that have been ordaining women for more than one generation leads directly into a discussion about the biblical texts and theological arguments used by opponents as well as proponents. At stake here is the character of the institution of Christianity. Will significant sectors of the religion continue to be led and shaped solely by men?

The first woman ordained by any major Christian denomination is generally acknowledged to have been Antoinette Brown in 1853. Brown was educated at Oberlin College and was ordained at a Congregational church in New York. Brown's ordination coincided somewhat with the first wave of feminism and took place in a denomination that had little or no national church structure in place setting policies and procedures for local congregations. This was likely a contributing factor to the milestone. At this time, other denominations with more defined structures began some discussions about the role of women in leading the church, but like the first wave of feminism, widespread public activism by women for leadership in Christian churches fell away in the early twentieth century.

By the early 1950s, coinciding with the just-emerging second wave of feminism, women began to more convincingly make the case that they were called to leadership in the Christian church, and they started gaining more access to the education often associated with credentialing church leaders. The paths for women into full leadership positions in churches were complicated, and so specifying dates when denominations began ordaining women often ignores events like the 1974 irregular ordination of eleven women in the Episcopal Church by a retired bishop in Philadelphia. It was irregular because the denomination did not officially ordain women at that time. This was a strategic move designed in part to push the issue, and the church officially began ordaining women in 1976.

In addition, Christian denominations are themselves complicated organizations often made up of predecessor churches, and so while Anna Howard Shaw was ordained in the Methodist Protestant Church in 1880, that church body later merged with other denominations that did not ordain women and became part of what is now the United Methodist Church. That denomination approved full ordination rights for women in 1956. In other denominations, women were approved for ordination, and then the right was either eroded or completely removed. Southern Baptist churches began ordaining women in 1964, but that practice began to be reversed by the denomination's passing various resolutions restricting women's work in the church throughout the 1980s and 1990s. "The Baptist Faith and Message," a comprehensive statement on the church's theological claims and positions on issues, was issued in 2000, and in it women were fully prohibited from seeking ordination.

These brief historical notes reveal that the process by which women have become ordained leaders in Christian churches is itself complicated. The theological arguments and interpretation of biblical texts on which the arguments center are also nuanced and in some places hotly contested. The fact that major parts of Christianity still do not ordain women, like the Roman Catholic Church and many independently organized evangelical and Bible churches, demonstrates that many people remain convinced by these arguments. Women think that they can be pastors on the basis of a number of factors, often independent of any official policy or document. To discuss this aspect of the topic, separating out personal discernment from the role of the community in confirming a call to ministry is important.

On a personal, individual and internal level, women think that they can be pastors because they believe that they have been called by the Spirit of God to leadership and service in the church. Discerning a call to ministry is an intensely

personal and often complicated process that women and men
have been navigating as long as there have been Christian
communities. On this level, there is little qualitative difference between women and men. The unique discernment experiences for women come when they try to reconcile their
internal sense of call to ministry with a church and a society
that either openly reject such a possibility or provide so few
models of women in ministry that they confront additional
barriers to recognizing and responding to the call that they
have discerned.

Discerning a call eventually brings an individual into
direct relationship with the Christian community and its
theological and biblical traditions. As history shows, the lasting acceptance of women in ordained church leadership positions is either relatively new or nonexistent in many Christian
denominations. Even fifty years of ordaining women is a
small amount of time compared with more than a millennium and three quarters of not really doing it and actively
opposing it. Traditional arguments against ordaining women
have varied across the centuries and across denominations,
but significant ones are these: Jesus chose only men to be his
twelve apostles. The Bible exhorts women not to teach and
have authority over men. As punishment for Eve's sin, woman
is made subject to man.

Women and men have responded to these arguments
with compelling cases for reinterpreting the biblical texts and
for reforming church tradition. John Wijngaards and Karen
Torjesen in their respective works on women in the early
church show that the early Christian church did not in fact
completely exclude women from church leadership positions.
Whether one looks to references in New Testament texts

themselves to women among the apostles or to references to women's speaking and teaching in Christian communities or to later Roman documents discussing the order of widows and their ministry, women clearly played leadership roles in the early church.

In addition, examining the logic of arguments such as the contention that Jesus chose twelve men to be his apostles presents questions: Why did he choose twelve? (His choice was a clear effort to invoke the twelve tribes of Israel.) Why did he choose men? (Jesus lived in a patriarchal culture when women had little public authority to speak and teach.) Careful study of texts like those in which Paul prohibits women from speaking in churches reveals specific contextual reasons for the prohibition: it was a temporary response to the threat of Gnostics and other groups to the cohesion of that early Christian community. Many denominations have been compelled to change on the basis of discussions like this. At the same time, many have rejected these arguments.

While many feminists would agree that if women want to become pastors, then they should have the same rights and access as men to the education and the process by which ordination occurs, other feminists would disagree. Their core argument is that putting women at the head of a patriarchal religion fails to actually reform the institution that is the problem in the first place. In fact, they argue that such a practice is dangerous and deceptive, allowing the patriarchal institution to present an inclusive face to the world while it continues to oppress and dehumanize.

In addition, not all women think that women can and should be pastors. Women as well as men can and do accept the teachings of Christian churches that reserve the most powerful and prestigious positions for men. This is because patriarchy is a system of beliefs and practices that privilege men over women, a system into which anyone, male or female, can buy. Nevertheless, as modern history shows, more Christian churches are accepting the fact that women can become pastors, priests, and bishops, changing the face of the religion by changing the character of the institution. In the twenty-first century, systematic exclusion of women from leadership positions simply because of their sex is something that finds fewer and fewer defenders.

Women think they can be pastors on the basis of their own internal sense of being called by the Spirit of God along with a faithful interpretation of biblical texts that has reformed the Christian tradition in the direction of inclusion.

SUGGESTED READING

Linda Belleville et al. *Two Views on Women in Ministry*. 2005.

Karen Jo Torjesen. *When Women Were Priests: Women's Leadership in the Early Church and the Scandal of their Subordination in the Rise of Christianity*. 1993.

John Wijngaards. *The Ordination of Women in the Catholic Church: Unmasking a Cuckoo's Egg Tradition*. 2001.

Conclusion

A new colleague asked me a great question when I was discussing this book with her: "What do you want people to do with all of this information now that they have it?" My extended answer to that question seems an important end to this work.

Christians can realize that their religious tradition is a complicated one, especially when it comes to the role and status of women, and can now appreciate the role that feminism has had and continues to have in improving the lives of women and men inside and outside the church. Feminists can realize that Christianity is more than an oppressive institution, and that it is a religion with a positive legacy for women and men that remains a powerful force worthy of activist engagement today.

What feminists and Christians do with this knowledge depends in large measure on their situation and their own context. For women who have been told by their Christian pastors that they should bear the cross of suffering in a violent relationship, this knowledge equips them to see a different Christian response to abuse and to free themselves from it. For men who demonize feminists and mock women, this knowledge allows them to understand how their sisters and mothers and friends are denigrated under patriarchy and to take responsibility for changing locker-room culture.

Church reading groups and their pastors might be inspired to examine the language that they use to talk about God on a daily and weekly basis in worship, prayer, and public communication. If language does not reflect the fullness and diversity of the human community, they may take steps to change it. Young third-wave feminist activists might be willing now to see how some Christians can be partners in advocating for federal marriage equality, debunking the popular misuse of God's word to discriminate against gay and lesbian Americans. They no longer need to accept the way the Bible is invoked by heterosexist political foes.

Feminist writers in the twenty-first century might now be willing and able to more directly engage with the complicated history and theology of Christianity. Christian scholars today might be less willing to assume that feminism is no longer relevant. Students might notice what area of dialogue between feminism and Christianity is most in need of attention today and research it further, adding their own voice to the emerging field of feminist theology.

In general, anyone who reads this book likely has some vested interest in either feminism or Christianity or both. That person knows what is missing, what needs greater elaboration, where more attention is demanded, and will participate in the ongoing construction of third-wave feminist theology. I look forward to seeing the results of those conversations and actions.

Questions and Answers

Chapter 1: Feminist Questions of Christianity

1. Why should feminists care about Christianity?

Feminism should reform Christianity to establish and maintain women's equal humanity while confronting patriarchy—a status-quo ideology that maintains male power over women.

2. How has Christianity been a problem for women?

Christianity is guilty of misunderstanding women, holding them back, and legitimating their abuse, so feminists must subject it to scrutiny and hold it accountable for failure or for renewal.

3. Has Christianity been oppressive only on the basis of gender?

The shameful Christian legacy of violence against and exploitation of other religious people and the earth is being overcome by faithful activism in which feminists can and should participate.

4. How has Christianity affected women's lives in a positive way?

Christianity has been good for women because of its theological vision of equality under a compassionate God and because of its

*historical and present practice of radical community organizing
and transformation led by women.*

5. How are feminists changing the fact that Christianity has
    been anti-feminist, if not anti-woman?

*Feminists are changing the fact that Christianity has been
anti-feminist and anti-woman through activism, scholarly engagement, and faithful participation that have resulted in denominational and biblical shifts toward inclusion.*

6. If Jesus was a feminist, and Paul was a misogynist, what's
    the real Christianity?

*While it is anachronistic to claim that Jesus was a feminist, and
too limiting to name Paul a misogynist, deeper knowledge about
each of the historical figures is simply part of the larger story of
the real Christianity.*

7. How do different Christian sects or denominations deal
    with women?

*Different Christian denominations deal with women in a variety
of ways from complete exclusion to complete inclusion in leadership roles; a corresponding diversity of ideas about women's
equality and humanity reveals that despite a bent toward justice
in Christianity, the religion continues to have loud and powerful
leaders insistent on preserving patriarchal power.*

8. Is Christianity better or worse for women than other
    religions?

*Christianity is incredibly similar to other religions when it comes
to women: A wide range of views and ways of treating women
have always been connected to an intricate set of historical and*

political factors that can completely affirm as well as completely
subordinate and mistreat women.

Chapter 2: Christian Questions of Feminism

1. Why should Christians care about feminism?

Christians should care about feminism because it brings the re-
ligion back to the root ideals of egalitarian human life glimpsed
in its early years, and because feminism has contributed to revi-
talizing the religion by advocating the leadership and scholarly
contributions of women.

2. Why don't feminists accept that the Bible teaches that men
   and women have different roles in creation, and that wives
   should submit to their husbands?

Feminists and Christians learn through closer historical, theo-
logical, and sociological examination that biblical texts and reli-
gious teachings against the full equality of men and women are
limited by their contexts in their ability to communicate truth.

3. Isn't feminism just a lot of whining, privileged, white
   women?

Feminism in the third wave is a global justice movement acting
on behalf of women's full equality at the intersection of race,
class, gender, and other aspects of identity—making it even more
relevant for a global Christianity in the twenty-first century.

4. Do feminists just want to turn patriarchy into a
   matriarchy?

Feminism's focus on women names the problem of sexism and
the reality of inequality in society and in the church, challeng-

ing a system that values and grants power to some people over others on the basis of unearned privileges.

5. How can a person be both Christian and feminist?

A person can be both Christian and feminist because the two identities share core commitments to human dignity and equality, justice among people, and sustainable relationships with the earth.

6. Are all feminists really lesbians? Doesn't feminism at least promote the sin of homosexuality?

Debunking assumptions about feminism as well as Christianity when it comes to homosexuality leads to a realistic challenge to the religious tradition that some denominations are meeting and others are battling.

7. Does feminism include goddess worship? If so, isn't it anti-Christian?

Feminism challenges Christianity to understand its history of suppressing concepts of a female deity as well as to open itself up to a rich storehouse of images and names for God that more fully represents human experience.

8. Why do women think they can be pastors?

Women think they can be pastors on the basis of their own internal sense of being called by the Spirit of God along with a faithful interpretation of biblical texts that has reformed the Christian tradition in the direction of inclusion.

Glossary

Abrahamic: a term used to refer to Judaism, Christianity, and Islam because of their common claims to Abraham as a founding ancestor.

Androcentric: centered on the male; describes a way of thinking in which male experience is taken as normal for all human beings.

Black liberation theology: a theological movement that talks about God and religion from the perspective of African American experience; originated with James Cone, *Black Theology and Black Power* (1969), and *A Black Theology of Liberation* (1970).

Canon: the list of accepted and authoritative books in a collection like the Bible; varies by Christian tradition; e.g., the Catholic canon differs from the Protestant canon.

Christianity: a religion based on the core belief that Jesus is the Christ, the messiah promised to deliver God's people from sin and death.

Denomination: any one of a number of sub-groups within Christianity, usually associated with Protestant groups.

Ecofeminism: a movement that integrates concerns for environmental justice with advocacy for women's equal humanity and recognizes the connection between the treatment of women and the treatment of the earth.

Environmental racism: the disproportionate effects of environmental destruction on poor people and people of color around the world.

Feminism: a worldview that criticizes sexism and patriarchy, and that advocates for the equal humanity of women.

First wave: metaphor used to describe the generation of feminists in the nineteenth century, whose main focus was obtaining for women in the United States the legal right to vote.

Gender: the socially constructed meaning attached to sex: social norming of the masculine and the feminine.

Heterosexism: prejudice against expressions of sexuality that are not heterosexual.

Heteronormative: presuming that heterosexuality is the only acceptable expression of human sexual interaction.

Homphobia: fear of homosexuality; fear of homosexuals.

Intersectional analysis: a way of thinking that pays attention to the multiple sources of privilege and oppression that affect everyone—especially race, class, gender, and sexuality.

Lesbian baiting: attempting to dissuade women from identifying with feminism and connecting with other women by calling them lesbians; works with the patriarchal assumption that being a lesbian is a negative thing.

Liberation theology: theology from the perspective of Latin American experiences of poverty and injustice; originated with the 1968 meetings of Latin American bishops in Medellín, Colombia, and the writings of Gustavo Gutiérrez.

Matriarchy: organization of a community giving women more power than men.

Matrilineal: describes a family system where naming and other inheritance characteristics follow the line of the mother.

Monotheism: belief in one God.

Misogyny: hatred of women.

Mujerista: one who does theology from the perspective of Hispanic women's experience.

Patriarchy: way of organizing the world in which men dominate women, in which associations with the male are superior to associations with the female.

Process philosophy: a school of thought based on a view that all levels of reality are organically related, in process, and not static; built on the foundational work of philosopher and mathematician Alfred North Whitehead.

Racism: prejudice against others based on race; a system that privileges one race over others.

Second wave: metaphor used to describe the generation of feminists active beginning in the middle of the twentieth century, whose main focus was on reproductive freedom, an equal-rights amendment, and educational equality for women.

Sex: term that refers to a person's biological makeup, usually male or female.

Sexism: prejudice against others based on sex and/or gender; a system that privileges one gender over others.

Sexuality: term used to describe a person's sexual interests and behaviors.

Third wave: metaphor used to describe the generation of feminists active in the twenty-first century who were raised during and with the benefits of second-wave feminism; works to include awareness of race, class, sexuality, age, ability, and many other factors that shape human identity.

Trinity/Triune: central Christian theological doctrine that understands the one God to exist in three forms: creator, redeemer, sanctifier / Father, Son, Holy Spirit.

Vatican II (Second Vatican Council): series of meetings from 1962 to 1965 wherein the Roman Catholic Church discussed and issued statements on a number of issues relevant to the church in the modern world.

Womanist: typically refers to black feminist women doing theology from their particular tridimensional race-class-gender experience; the term comes from Alice Walker's poetic definition in the preface to *In Search of Our Mother's Gardens* (1983).

Bibliography

Ahmed, Leila. *Women and Gender in Islam: Historical Roots of a Modern Debate*. New Haven: Yale University Press, 1993.

Alpert, Rebecca. "Same-Sex Marriage and the Law." Online: http://www.shalomctr.org/node/3/.

Attridge, Harold, general editor. *The HarperCollins Study Bible: New Revised Standard Version, including the Apocryphal/Deuterocanonical Books*. Fully revised and updated. Student edition. San Francisco: HarperSanFrancisco, 2006.

Bagley, Kate, and Kathleen McIntosh, editors. *Women's Studies in Religion: A Multicultural Reader*. Upper Saddle River, NJ: Pearson/Prentice Hall, 2007.

Barnett, Victoria. "The Role of the Churches: Compliance and Confrontation." In *The Holocaust and the Christian World: Reflections on the Past, Challenges for the Future*, edited by Carol Rittner et al., 55–58. New York: Continuum, 2000.

Baskin, Judith R., editor. *Jewish Women in Historical Perspective*. 2nd ed. Detroit: Wayne State University Press, 1998.

Baumgardner, Jennifer, and Amy Richards. *Manifesta: Young Women, Feminism, and the Future*. New York: Farrar, Straus and Giroux, 2000.

Beauvoir, Simone de. *The Second Sex*. Translated and edited by H. M. Parshley. 1949. Reprint, New York: Vintage, 1989.

Belleville, Linda L. et al. *Two Views on Women in Ministry*. Edited by James R. Beck. Rev. ed. Counterpoints. Grand Rapids: Zondervan, 2005.

Berkes, Howard. "Gender Barrier Persists at Vancouver Olympics." *All Things Considered*, National Public Radio, December 29, 2008. Online: http://www.npr.org/templates/story/story.php?storyId=98593877/.

Bohn, Carole R. "Dominion to Rule: The Roots and Consequences of a Theology of Ownership." In *Christianity, Patriarchy, and Abuse: A Feminist Critique*, edited by Joanne Carlson Brown and Carole R. Bohn, 105–16. Cleveland: Pilgrim, 1989.

Boswell, John. *Christianity, Social Tolerance, and Homosexuality: Gay People in Western Europe from the Beginning of the Christian Era to the Fourteenth Century*. Chicago: University of Chicago Press, 1980.

Bréhier, Louis. "Crusades." In *The Catholic Encyclopedia*. Vol. 4. New York: Robert Appleton Company, 1908. Online: http://www.newadvent.org/cathen/04543c.htm/.

Brown, Dan. *The Da Vinci Code: A Novel*. New York: Doubleday, 2003.

Brown, Joanne Carlson, and Carole R. Bohn, editors. *Christianity, Patriarchy, and Abuse: A Feminist Critique*. Cleveland: Pilgrim, 1989.

Bruyneel, Sally, and Alan G. Padgett. *Introducing Christianity*. Maryknoll, NY: Orbis, 2003.

Buddha Dharma Education Association. "Buddhism and Women." Online: http://www.buddhanet.net/e-learning/history/women.htm/.

Bush, Laura. "Radio Address by Mrs. Bush." November 17, 2001. Online: http://www.presidency.ucsb.edu/ws/index.php?pid=24992/.

Bushnell, Katharine. *God's Word to Women*. 1921. Reprint, Minneapolis: Christians for Biblical Equality, 2003.

Christ, Carol P. *She Who Changes: Re-imagining the Divine in the World*. New York: Palgrave Macmillan, 2004.

———. *Rebirth of the Goddess: Finding Meaning in Feminist Spirituality*. Reading, MA: Addison-Wesley, 1997.

Christ, Carol P., and Judith Plaskow, editors. *Womanspirit Rising: A Feminist Reader in Religion*. San Francisco: HarperSanFrancisco, 1992.

———. *Weaving the Visions: New Patterns in Feminist Spirituality*. San Francisco: Harper & Row, 1989.

Clark, Elizabeth A., and Herbert Richardson, editors. *Women and Religion: The Original Sourcebook of Women in Christian Thought*, 119–43. San Francisco: HarperSanFrancisco, 1996.

———. "Woman as Witch: Witchcraft Persecutions in the Old and New World." In *Women and Religion: The Original Sourcebook of Women in Christian Thought*, edited by Elizabeth A. Clark and Herbert Richardson, 119–43. Rev. ed. San Francisco: HarperSanFrancisco, 1996.

Clements, Sandra. "Submission." Online: http://www.godswordtowomen.org/submission.htm/.

Clifford, Anne M. *Introducing Feminist Theology*. Maryknoll, NY: Orbis, 2001.

Coleman, Monica A., et al. "Roundtable Discussion: Must I Be a Womanist?" *Journal of Feminist Studies in Religion* 22 (2006) 85–134.

Corbett, Christianne et al. *Where the Girls Are: The Facts about Gender Equity in Education.* Washington DC: American Association of University Women, 2008. Online: http://www.aauw.org/About/newsroom/upload/whereGirlsAre.pdf/.

Daly, Mary. *Beyond God the Father: Toward a Philosophy of Women's Liberation.* Boston: Beacon, 1973.

————. *The Church and the Second Sex,* with the feminist post-Christian introduction and new archaic afterwords by the author. Boston: Beacon, 1985.

————. *Gyn/Ecology: The Metaethics of Radical Feminism.* Boston: Beacon, 1978.

————. "Sin Big." *The New Yorker,* February 26 & March 4, 1996, 76–84.

————. "The Women's Movement: An Exodus Community." *Religious Education* 67 (1972) 327–33.

"Ebenezer/herchurch Lutheran, San Francisco, ELCA." Web page. Online: http://www.herchurch.org/.

Eisen, Arnold M. "Chancellor-Elect Eisen's Letter to the JTS Community." Online: http://www.jtsa.edu/Conservative_Judaism/The_Halakhic_Status_of_Homosexual_Behavior/Eisen_Letter_-_Ordination.xml/.

Eisler, Riane. *The Chalice and the Blade: Our History, Our Future.* San Francisco: Harper & Row, 1987.

Episcopal Church USA. Web site. Online: http://ecusa.anglican.org/.

Esposito, John L., and Daria Mogahed. *Who Speaks for Islam? What A Billion Muslims Really Think.* New York: Gallup Press, 2007.

Evangelical Lutheran Church in America. "Abortion." Online: http://www.elca.org/What-We-Believe/Social-Issues/Social-Statements/Abortion.aspx/

————. Web site. Online: http://www.elca.org/.

Freedman, Estelle B. *No Turning Back: The History of Feminism and the Future of Women.* New York: Ballantine, 2002.

————. *Feminism, Sexuality, and Politics: Essays.* Gender and American Culture. Chapel Hill: University of North Carolina Press, 2006.

Gage, Frances Dana. "Ain't I a Woman?" *Anti-Slavery Standard,* May 2, 1863. Online: http://www.sojournertruth.org/Library/Speeches/AintIAWoman.htm/.

Gage, Matilda Joslyn. *Woman, Church and State.* Classics in Women's Studies. Amherst, MA: Humanity Books, 2002.

Gilkes, Cheryl Townsend. *If It Wasn't for the Women: Black Women's Experience and Womanist Culture in Church and Community.* Maryknoll, NY: Orbis, 2001.

Gold, Victor Roland et al. *An Inclusive-Language Lectionary.* 3 vols. Philadelphia: Westminster, 1983–1985.

Graham, Elaine. "Feminist Theology, Northern." In *The Blackwell Companion to Political Theology* edited by William T. Cavanaugh and Peter Scott, 210–26. Blackwell Companions to Religion. Malden, MA: Blackwell, 2004.

Grant, Jacquelyn. *White Women's Christ and Black Women's Jesus: Feminist Christology and Womanist Response.* American Academy of Religion Academy Series 64. Atlanta: Scholars, 1989.

Grant, Robert M. *Irenaeus of Lyons.* The Early Church Fathers. London: Routledge, 1998.

Grenz, Stanley J., with Denise Muir Kjesbo. *Women in the Church: A Biblical Theology of Women in Ministry.* Downers Grove, IL: InterVarsity, 1995.

Grimke, Sarah, and Elizabeth Ann Bartlett. *Letters on the Equality of the Sexes and Other Essays.* Edited with an introduction by Elizabeth Ann Bartlett. New Haven: Yale University Press, 1988.

Gross, Rita, and Rosemary Radford Ruether. *Religious Feminism and the Future of the Planet: A Christian-Buddhist Conversation.* New York: Continuum, 2001.

Gudorf, Christine E. "Contraception and Abortion in Roman Catholicism." In *Sacred Rights: The Case for Contraception and Abortion in World Religions,* edited by Daniel C. Maguire, 55–78. New York: Oxford University Press, 2003.

Gutiérrez, Gustavo. "Toward a Theology of Liberation." (1968) In *Liberation Theology: A Documentary History,* edited by Alfred T. Hennelly, 62–76. Maryknoll, NY: Orbis, 1995.

Harvard Pluralism Project. *Women's Networks Initiative.* Online: http://www.pluralism.org/women/.

Helminiak, Daniel A. *What the Bible Really Says about Homosexuality.* Tajique, NM: Alamo, 2000.

Henold, Mary J. *Catholic and Feminist: The Surprising History of the American Catholic Feminist Movement.* Chapel Hill: University of North Carolina Press, 2008.

Heschel, Susannah, editor. *On Being a Jewish Feminist: A Reader.* New York: Schocken, 1995.

Hilkert, Mary Catherine. *Speaking with Authority: Catherine of Siena and the Voices of Women Today.* Rev. ed. New York: Paulist, 2008.

Hill, Anita C., and Leo Treadway. "Rituals of Healing: Ministry with and on behalf of Gay and Lesbian People." In *Lift Every Voice: Constructing Christian Theologies from the Underside,* edited by Susan Brooks Thistlethwaite and Mary Potter Engel, 237–50. Rev. ed. Maryknoll, NY: Orbis, 1998.

Holladay, Jennifer R. "Sexism in the Civil Rights Movement: A Discussion Guide." Southern Poverty Law Center (August 2000). Online: http://www.tolerance.org/teach/activities/activity.jsp?cid=159/.

The Holy See (the Roman Catholic Church). Web site. Online: http://www.vatican.va/.

hooks, bell. *Feminism is for Everybody: Passionate Politics.* Cambridge, MA: South End, 2000.

———. *Feminist Theory: From Margin to Center.* 2nd ed. South End Press Classics 5. Cambridge, MA: South End, 2000.

I.R.I.N. "Iraq: Widow Numbers Rise," The U.N. Office for the Coordination of Humanitarian Affairs. Online: http://www.irinnews.org/Report.aspx?ReportId=26320/.

Isasi–Díaz, Ada María. *En la Lucha = In the Struggle: Elaborating a Mujerista Theology; A Hispanic Women's Liberation Theology.* Minneapolis: Fortress, 1993.

Japinga, Lynn. *Feminism and Christianity: An Essential Guide.* Abingdon Essential Guides. Nashville: Abingdon, 1999.

Johnson, Elizabeth. *She Who Is: The Mystery of God in Feminist Theological Discourse.* New York: Crossroad, 1992.

Jones, Darice. "Falling off the Tightrope onto a Bed of Feathers." In *Women's Studies in Religion: A Multicultural Reader,* edited by Kate Bagley and Kathleen McIntosh, 137–43. Upper Saddle River, NJ: Pearson Prentice Hall, 2007.

Jule, Allyson, and Bettina Tate Pederson, editors. *Being Feminist, Being Christian: Essays from Academia.* New York: Palgrave Macmillan, 2008.

Keller, Catherine. "The Apophasis of Gender: A Fourfold Unsaying of Feminist Theology." *Journal of the American Academy of Religion* 76 (2008) 905–33.

Kepnes, Steven. "Adam/Eve: From Rabbinic to Scriptural Anthropology." *Journal of Scriptural Reasoning* 4 (2004). Online: http://etext.lib.virginia.edu/journals/ssr/issues/volume4/number2/ssr04_02_e01.html/.

Khan, Noor. "10 Taliban Arrested in School Girl Acid Attack." *The Globe and Mail,* November 25, 2008. Online: *http://www.awid.org/eng/Issues-and-Analysis/Library/10-Taliban-arrested-in-school-girl-acid-attack/(language)/eng-GB.*

Kosmin, Barry A., et al. "The American Religious Identification Survey." (2001). The Graduate Center at the City University of New York. Online: http://www.gc.cuny.edu/faculty/research_studies/aris.pdf/.

Kramer, Heinrich, and Jacob Sprenger. *The "Malleus Maleficarum."* Translated by Montague Summers. New York: Cosimo Classics, 2007.

Lorde, Audre. "Age, Race, Class, and Sex." In *Sister Outsider: Essays and Speeches*, 114–23. Women's Studies. Freedom, CA: Crossing, 1996.

———. "The Master's Tools Will Never Dismantle the Master's House." In *Sister Outsider: Essays and Speeches*, 110–13. Women's Studies. Freedom, CA: Crossing, 1996.

Luther, Martin. "On the Jews and Their Lies." (1543) In *Luther's Works* 47:123–306. Edited by Frank Sherman. Philadelphia: Fortress, 1971.

———. "The Freedom of a Christian." (1520) In *Luther's Works* 31:333–77. Edited by Harold J. Grimm. Philadelphia: Fortress, 1957.

Maguire, Daniel C. *Sacred Rights: The Case for Contraception and Abortion in World Religions*. New York: Oxford University Press, 2000.

McDougall, Joy Ann. "Feminist Theology for a New Generation." *The Christian Century*, July 26, 2005, 20–25.

Menon-Sen, Kalyani, and A. K. Shiva Kumar. "Women in India: How Free? How Equal?" Office of the Resident Coordinator in India, United Nations. Online: http://www.un.org.in/wii.htm/.

Migliore, Daniel L. *Faith Seeking Understanding: An Introduction to Christian Theology*. Grand Rapids: Eerdmans, 2004.

Morton, Nelle, "The Goddess as Metaphoric Image." In *Women's Studies in Religion: A Multicultural Reader*, edited by Kate Bagley and Kathleen McIntosh, PAGES. New Jersey: Pearson, 2007.

Naughton, Phillipe. "Elisabeth Fritzl Tells of Father's Cruelty." *The Times Online*, September 10, 2008. Online: http://www.timesonline.co.uk/tol/news/world/europe/article4722938.ece/.

Newsom, Carol A. and Sharon H. Ringe, editors. *Women's Bible Commentary*. Expanded edition. Louisville: Westminster John Knox, 1998.

Pagels, Elaine. *Adam, Eve, and the Serpent*. New York: Random House, 1988.

Paul VI. *Humanae Vitae* (*On the Regulation of Birth*). Online: http://www.vatican.va/holy_father/paul_vi/encyclicals/documents/hf_p-vi_enc_25071968_humanae-vitae_en.html/.

Pius XI. *Casti Connubii* (*On Christian Marriage*). Online: http://www.vatican.va/holy_father/pius_xi/encyclicals/documents/hf_p-xi_enc_31121930_casti-connubii_en.html/.

Plaskow, Judith. *Standing Again at Sinai: Judaism from a Feminist Perspective*. San Francisco: HarperCollins, 1991.

Polaski, Sandra Hack. *A Feminist Introduction to Paul*. Atlanta: Chalice, 2005.

Powell, Mark Allan. *Fortress Introduction to the Gospels*. Minneapolis: Fortress, 1998.

Presbyterian Church USA. "Response to Inclusive Language." Online: http://www.pcusa.org/theologyandworship/issues/inclusive.htm/.

————. Presbyterian Church USA. Web site. Online: http://www.pcusa .org/.

Rhoads, David. *The Challenge of Diversity: The Witness of Paul and the Gospels*. Minneapolis: Fortress, 1996.

Riley, Gregory J. *One Jesus, Many Christs: How Jesus Inspired Not One True Christianity, but Many; the Truth about Christian Origins*. 1997. Reprint, Minneapolis: Fortress, 2000.

Rittner, Carol, et al., editors. *The Holocaust and the Christian World: Reflections on the Past, Challenges for the Future*. New York: Continuum, 2000.

Rivers, Caryl, and Rosalind Chait Barnett. "The Myth of the Boy Crisis." *The Washington Post* April 9, 2006. Online: http://www.washingtonpost .com/wp–dyn/content/article/2006/04/07/AR2006040702025.html/.

Robinson, Marcus. "On Women's Rights." *Anti–Slavery Bugle* (June 25, 1851). Online: http://www.sojournertruth.org/Library/Speeches/ Default.htm/.

Ruether, Rosemary Radford. *Gaia & God: An Ecofeminist Theology of Earth Healing*. San Francisco: HarperCollins, 1992.

————. *Religion and Sexism: Images of Woman in the Jewish and Christian Traditions*. 1974. Reprint. Eugene, OR: Wipf & Stock, 1998.

————. *Sexism and God-Talk: Toward a Feminist Theology*. Boston: Beacon, 1983.

————. *Sexism and God-Talk: Toward a Feminist Theology*, with a new introduction. 10th anniversary edition. Boston: Beacon, 1993.

————. *Women-Church: Theology & Practice of Feminist Liturgical Communities*. San Francisco: Harper & Row, 1985.

Ruether, Rosemary Radford, and Rosemary Skinner Keller, general editors. *Women and Religion in America: A Documentary History*. 3 vols. San Francisco: Harper & Row, 1981–1986.

Russell, Letty M., and J. Shannon Clarkson, editors. *Dictionary of Feminist Theologies*. Louisville: Westminster John Knox, 1996.

Russell, Letty M., et al, editors. *Inheriting Our Mothers Gardens: Feminist Theology in Third World Perspective*. Louisville: Westminster, 1988.

Sample, Ian. "Sex Objects: Pictures Shift Men's View of Women." *The Guardian*, February 16, 2009. Online: http://www.guardian.co.uk/ science/2009/feb/16/sex–object–photograph/.

Saiving Goldstein, Valerie. "The Human Situation: A Feminine View." *Journal of Religion* 40:2 (1960) 100–112.

Schearing, Linda S., et al., editors. *Eve and Adam: Jewish, Christian, and Muslim Readings on Genesis and Gender*. Bloomington: Indiana University Press, 1999.

Schmidt, Frederick W., Jr. *A Still Small Voice: Women, Ordination, and the Church*. Women and Gender in North American Religions. Syracuse: Syracuse University Press, 1996.

Schüssler Fiorenza, Elisabeth. *In Memory of Her: A Feminist Theological Reconstruction of Christian Origins*. New York: Crossroad, 1983.

————. *Jesus: Miriam's Child, Sophia's Prophet; Critical Issues in Feminist Christology*. New York: Continuum, 1995.

Seager, Joni. *The Penguin Atlas of Women in the World*. 4th ed. New York: Penguin, 2008.

Shaw, Susan M., and Janet Lee, editors. *Women's Voices, Feminist Visions: Classic and Contemporary Readings*. 2nd edition. Boston: McGraw-Hill, 2004.

Siker, Jeffrey S., editor. *Homosexuality in the Church: Both Sides of the Debate*. Louisville: Westminster John Knox, 1994.

Sommers, Christina Hoff. "The War against Boys." *The Atlantic*, May 2000. Online: http://www.theatlantic.com/doc/200005/war-against-boys/.

Southern Baptist Convention. "The Baptist Faith and Message" (2000). Online: http://www.sbc.net/bfm/bfm2000.asp/.

Southern Baptist Convention: http://www.sbc.net/.

Stanton, Elizabeth Cady. *The Woman's Bible: A Classic Feminist Perspective*. Mineola, NY: Dover, 2003.

Stowe, Harriet Beecher. "Sojourner Truth, The Libyan Sibyl." *The Atlantic Monthly*, April 1863. Online: http://www.sojournertruth.org/Library/Archive/LibyanSibyl.htm/.

Tertullian, *De culto feminarum* [*On Female Fashion*]. Online: http://www.tertullian.org/works/de_cultu_feminarum.htm/.

Thistlethwaite, Susan Brooks, and Mary Potter Engel, editors. *Lift Every Voice: Constructing Christian Theology from the Underside*. Rev. ed. Maryknoll, NY: Orbis, 1998.

Tjaden, Patricia, and Nancy Thoennes. *Extent, Nature, and Consequences of Intimate Partner Violence*. Washington DC: U. S. Department of Justice, Office of Justice Programs, National Institute of Justice, 2000. Online: http://www.ncjrs.gov/pdffiles1/nij/181867.pdf/.

Torjesen, Karen Jo. *When Women Were Priests: Women's Leadership in the Early Church and the Scandal of their Subordination in the Rise of Christianity*. San Francisco: HarperSanFrancisco, 1993.

Townes, Emilie M., editor. *A Troubling in My Soul: Womanist Perspectives on Evil and Suffering*. The Bishop Henry McNeal Turner Studies in North American Black Religion 6. Maryknoll, NY: Orbis, 1993.

————. *Womanist Justice, Womanist Hope*. American Academy of Religion Academy Series 79. Atlanta: Scholars, 1993.

Trible, Phyllis. *God and the Rhetoric of Sexuality*. Overtures to Biblical Theology. Philadelphia: Fortress, 1978.

————. *Texts of Terror: Literary-Feminist Readings of Biblical Narratives*. Overtures to Biblical Theology. Philadelphia: Fortress, 1984.

United Church of Christ. Web site. Online: http://www.ucc.org/.

United Nations Population Fund. "Facts About Safe Motherhood." Online: http://www.unfpa.org/mothers/facts.htm/.

U.S. Census Bureau. "Household Income Rises, Poverty Rate Declines, Number of Uninsured Up." August 28, 2007. Online: http://www.census.gov/Press-Release/www/releases/archives/income_wealth/010583.html/.

Vatican Council, Second. *Declaration on the Relationship of the Church to Non-Christian Religions (Nostra Aetate)*. Online: http://www.vatican.va/archive/hist_councils/ii_vatican_council/documents/vat-ii_decl_19651028_nostra-aetate_en.html.

Von Garnier, Katja, director. *Iron-Jawed Angels*, starring Hilary Swank, Frances O'Connor, et al. DVD. New York: HBO Video, 2004.

Wadud, Amina. *Quran and Woman: Rereading the Sacred Text from a Woman's Perspective*. New York: Oxford University Press, 1999.

Walker, Alice. *In Search of Our Mothers' Gardens: Womanist Prose*. San Diego: Harcourt Brace Jovanovich, 1983.

Walker, Williston. *A History of the Christian Church*. 3rd rev. ed. by Robert T. Handy. New York: Scribners, 1970.

White, Lynn Townsend, Jr. "The Historical Roots of Our Ecologic Crisis." *Science* 155 (1967) 1203–7.

Wijngaards, John. *The Ordination of Women in the Catholic Church: Unmasking a Cuckoo's Egg Tradition*. New York, Continuum, 2001.

Williams, Delores S. *Sisters in the Wilderness: The Challenge of Womanist God-Talk*. Maryknoll, NY: Orbis, 1993.

Wooden, Cindy. "Attempts to Ordain Women Means Instant Excommunication." *The Catholic Register*, June 5, 2008. Online: http://www.catholicregister.org/content/view/1897/849/.

World Council of Churches. "Who Are We?" Online: http://www.oikoumene.org/en/who-are-we.html/.